Mastering

GMRS Radio

Comprehensive User Guide to Unlocking the Full
Potential of General Mobile Radio Service with Expert
Tips, Techniques, and Real-World Applications

Elior Weston

Table of Contents

Chapter 1

Introduction to GMRS Radios

Understanding GMRS Radio Communication

Effective communication can be crucial in survival scenarios, potentially saving lives. Thus, having reliable communication tools is vital for safety and planning, especially when venturing into the wilderness or facing unforeseen emergencies. General Mobile Radio Service (GMRS) radios serve as robust tools facilitating communication in such situations.

Understanding the nature of GMRS radios is essential before considering their use in survival scenarios. GMRS is a legally recognized radio service in the United States, operating within the UHF band. Unlike Family Radio Service (FRS) radios, GMRS radios offer an extended range, making them ideal for emergencies and outdoor excursions. However, it is imperative to obtain a GMRS license from the Federal Communications Commission (FCC) to utilize GMRS radios properly. Below is a breakdown of the different categories of how the GMRS radio communication is typically used;

Emergency Communication Plan

Before embarking on any expedition, for instance, to the desert, it is important to establish a comprehensive emergency communication plan. This plan should include:

- **Designating communication lines:** Select specific GMRS channels for emergency contact. Channels 1–7 are shared with FRS and suitable for short-range communication, while channels 15–22 are preferable for longer-range communication

- **Continuous channel monitoring:** Designate an individual within your group to monitor the radio consistently, especially during critical moments.

- Setting up emergency codes: Develop predetermined emergency codes or signals to convey important information swiftly and efficiently.

Proper Utilization of GMRS Radio

In survival situations, your ability to operate a radio (the GMRS radio communication in this case) is paramount. To optimize the functionality of your GMRS radio, adhere to the following guidelines:

- **Ensure fully charged batteries or carry additional batteries:** For prolonged survival scenarios, consider investing in small solar chargers or hand-crank chargers to maintain radio functionality.
- **Practice radio discipline:** Convey messages succinctly and clearly. Use concise language to transmit crucial information effectively.
- **Active listening**: Remain attentive to incoming transmissions when not transmitting. Vital information may be relayed, necessitating prompt attention.
- **Monitor signal strength:** Regularly monitor the radio's signal strength indicator to determine the need for repositioning to attain better reception.

Dedicated Channels for Emergency Situations

Although GMRS radios offer multiple channels, it is advisable to allocate specific channels solely for emergencies:

- **Emergency channel**: Designate a single GMRS channel exclusively for emergency communications. Reserve this channel solely for distress calls and requests for assistance.

- **Group channel:** Allocate a separate channel for your survival team to facilitate regular communication. Utilize this channel for coordinating activities, exchanging information, and maintaining group cohesion.

- **Scanning mode**: Configure your radios to scan various stations, including weather and emergency channels, to stay informed and receive critical updates.

Emergency Protocol

Understanding when and how to utilize your GMRS radio during emergencies is paramount for survival:

- **Mayday calls**: In emergency situations, utilize the designated emergency channel (e.g., GMRS channel 16) to transmit a "Mayday" distress call. Clearly state your location, the nature of the emergency, and the number of individuals involved. Repeat the distress call at regular intervals.

- **Utilize safety signals:** Familiarize yourself with universal distress signals such as the international SOS signal (three short, three long, three short) and Morse code for SOS (...—...). Employ these signals if necessary.

Monitoring Weather Conditions

Staying abreast of weather updates is crucial for survival, as weather conditions can significantly impact your well-being. GMRS radios can receive NOAA weather reports on certain stations.

Ensure these stations are programmed into your radios and regularly listen for weather updates and alerts.

Considerations Regarding Range

Understanding the effective range of your GMRS radios is essential. The range is influenced by terrain, obstacles, and radio power output. In survival scenarios, elevation, open terrain, or the use of repeaters can significantly extend communication range.

Integration of SOS Beacons and GPS

Some modern GMRS radios feature built-in SOS signals and GPS functionality, offering invaluable assistance during emergencies. Familiarize yourself with these features and ensure they are included in your emergency gear.

Signaling and Antennas

Beyond voice communication, GMRS radios can serve as signaling devices:

- **Whistles:** Carry a whistle to produce clear, audible signals over long distances.

- **Antennas**: Learn to extend and adjust the antenna for optimal signal transmission and reception. In some cases, improvising antennas, such as wire dipoles, can enhance signal range.

Practice and Familiarization

Before you venture into remote locations, dedicate time to practice and familiarize yourself and your group members with GMRS radio operation. Proficiency in equipment usage minimizes errors and confusion during emergencies, enhancing overall safety.

History and Evolution of GMRS Technology

In the late 1940s, a significant shift occurred in the realm of communication technology as CB radios began to emerge, operating within the UHF band. Al Gross's establishment of the Citizens Radio Corporation had a profound impact on the world of portable communication devices, leading to their widespread use among various user groups. The durability and user-friendly nature of class B handheld radios were especially attractive to farmers and maritime users, showcasing the adaptability of CB technology in meeting distinct communication requirements. During this era, the categorization of CB radios into Class A and Class B showcased the varied needs of radio users. Class A radios were known for their impressive power output and strong transmission capabilities, making them a popular choice among users. On the other hand, Class B radios were designed for specific applications, offering a smaller size and lower power consumption. This dual-class system set the stage for future developments in radio spectrum management and regulatory frameworks.

In the 1960s, the UHF band underwent a significant reallocation, leading to a need for a complete overhaul of radio communication standards and equipment design. With the adoption of 25 kHz channels, there was a significant improvement in spectrum utilization. This allowed for the deployment of a larger number of communication channels within the same frequency band, resulting in more efficient communication. The reliability and performance of CB radios were greatly improved by technological advancements in transmitter design and modulation techniques. As a result, these radios became essential tools in various industries. In the 1970s, there were notable shifts in the regulatory landscape to adapt to the changing communication needs and advancements in technology. The changes made to power levels and spectrum allocation demonstrate an increasing understanding of the crucial role that radio communication plays in promoting economic development and ensuring public safety. The distinction between CB Class A and Class B established the foundation for the future shift to GMRS and FRS, paving the way for more customized communication services designed for specific user groups.

The transformation of the radio service into GMRS in 1987 was a significant turning point in the development of two-way communication technology. The consolidation of various radio services into the GMRS umbrella resulted in more efficient regulatory oversight and improved communication among radio users. The FCC's decision to eliminate business licenses and implement a 10-year license term demonstrates their dedication to enhancing spectrum management efficiency and ensuring fair access to communication resources. The expansion of GMRS in 2017 marked a noteworthy milestone in the continuous development of radio communication standards and protocols. The incorporation of short data messaging applications and the inclusion of channels in the 467 MHz band broadened the usefulness and adaptability of GMRS, allowing users to utilize advanced communication features for an improved understanding of the situation and operational effectiveness. The FRS service definition was revised and hybrid FRS/GMRS radios were introduced, indicating a convergence of communication technologies and regulatory frameworks.

The regulatory restrictions imposed in 2019 highlighted the significance of safeguarding the integrity and security of communication networks. Through the prohibition of dual-mode radios capable of operating on both GMRS and FRS frequencies, regulators aimed to reduce the potential for interference and prevent unauthorized access to licensed spectrum. The licensing process has been refined and application fees have been reduced, which demonstrates a commitment to improving administrative procedures and ensuring better compliance with regulatory requirements.

The impact of GMRS on society goes beyond conventional limits, covering a diverse range of uses that include public safety, emergency response, commercial operations, and recreational activities. With the rapid advancement of communication technology, GMRS is positioned to become a vital tool in enabling smooth connectivity and the exchange of information across various sectors. The future of GMRS depends on ongoing advancements in radio technology, regulatory frameworks, and spectrum management practices. These factors are crucial in maintaining the effectiveness and relevance of GMRS in a rapidly evolving communication landscape.

Importance and Applications of GMRS Radios

General Mobile Radio Service (GMRS) Radio is a bidirectional radio technology that enables dependable and unambiguous communication within a designated frequency band. People and organizations use GMRS radios for various reasons, including responding to emergencies, going on outdoor excursions, and attending community activities. Below are some of the advantages and how you can apply the GMRS radios;

Long-Term Coverage

Increased Coverage

The increased range of GMRS radio makes long-distance communication possible, which is a major benefit. With their increased power output, GMRS radios can cover more ground than regular walkie-talkies. This is why GMRS radios are perfect for long-distance communication, which is essential for outdoor pursuits like hunting, camping, and trekking.

Ability to Communicate in Rural Areas

When mobile phone service is spotty or nonexistent in more remote places, GMRS radios come in handy. Without the need to depend on cellular networks, GMRS radios provide a dependable way to communicate, whether you are on a distant farm or adventuring in the woods. Those who work in agriculture, the outdoors, or emergency services who need to remain connected in places with little infrastructure may find this to be quite helpful.

Minimizing Interference

Privacy Codes

The ability to filter out other users' undesirable interference is a feature of GMRS radios called privacy codes, subchannels, or privacy tones. To prevent users on the same channel from overhearing one another's talks, privacy codes function by allocating a unique subchannel to each user. In busy places or when several groups are utilizing GMRS radios at the same time, this guarantees private and secure communication.

Variety of Available Channels

With GMRS radios, users may choose from a variety of channels to find the one that works best for their communication requirements. To avoid interference and ensure their connection is clear and dependable, users should choose a less crowded channel. The ability to choose from a wide variety of channels gives GMRS radios a highly adaptable means of communication.

Alternative Frequencies

GMRS radios are country- and region-specific, meaning they operate on different frequency bands. By adjusting these frequency settings, users may choose a channel that works best in their area. By providing customers with a variety of frequencies, GMRS radios guarantee maximum performance and clear communication, whether it is in the UHF band or VHF band.

Licensing

Requirements for Licensing

One must possess a current FCC (Federal Communications Commission) license in order to lawfully use GMRS radios. The responsible and effective use of the frequencies is ensured by this license, which permits people and enterprises to use GMRS radio equipment. The advantage here of using this is that the General Mobile Radio Service (GMRS) license is easy to get and grants the bearer and their immediate family members the right to use GMRS radios for both personal and professional usage.

License Fee

One advantage of the GMRS is that the GMRS license may be obtained for a reasonable price, allowing it to be used by many people. At the time this article was written, the FCC had a set price for a GMRS license that was good for 10 years. With this affordable license option, companies and individuals may take advantage of GMRS radios without going into debt.

Versatility

Application in Emergencies

When it comes to emergencies, GMRS radios are lifesavers. Individuals in need may rely on GMRS radios as a lifeline when more conventional forms of communication are ineffective. A GMRS radio provides a dependable mode of communication that may save lives in various situations, including search and rescue operations, emergency medical care coordination, and natural catastrophes. As a crucial component of disaster readiness, GMRS radios provide longer range, interference reduction capabilities, and interoperability with other emergency communication systems.

Applications for Personal and Business Uses

There is a vast array of personal and professional uses for GMRS radios beyond emergency scenarios. To ensure their loved ones' safety while enjoying outdoor activities, families may utilize GMRS radios to stay connected. Construction firms and event planners are just two examples of the types of businesses that might benefit from GMRS radios in terms of increased productivity and better collaboration. Both professional and personal communication may benefit from GMRS radios due to their adaptability and user-friendliness.

Illustration of GMRS Radio Communication being used for personal communication in a car

Compatibility

To facilitate communication with other radio systems, GMRS radios are built to be interoperable with FRS (Family Radio Service) radios and some maritime VHF radios. Because of this interoperability, users of various radio systems may communicate with one another without any hitches. The interoperability of GMRS radios makes communication straightforward and efficient, whether you are using it to talk with someone using a compatible FRS radio or to coordinate with maritime VHF users in coastal locations.

Durability and Dependability

Outdoor and industrial applications are no match for GMRS radios. A lot of models can resist dust, water, and even very hot or cold conditions since they are tough and waterproof. Because of their resilience, GMRS radios are dependable in even the most extreme settings, making them ideal for those who work outdoors, in emergency services, or in industries that face unique challenges.

Money Saving

The cost-effectiveness of GMRS radios is compared to alternative communication solutions. They don't need costly infrastructure or regular service costs, and they have a modest starting price. After the license is acquired, GMRS radios do not incur any more fees, making them a cost-effective long-term communication option for both people and enterprises.

Specifications and Features

Integration of Contemporary Technology

GMRS radios have made use of new technologies to improve their performance and usability. More recent versions are more adaptable and easy to use than older ones because of features like built-in GPS, Bluetooth, and voice activation. Thanks to these innovations, GMRS radios are still one of the most cutting-edge forms of contemporary communication.

Metrological Abilities

Some GMRS radios have the ability to send out weather alerts, so people can know when bad weather is on the way. The National Weather Service may send out alerts to these radios, so you can get up-to-the-minute information on weather warnings, watches, and advisories. Those who like spending time outside will find this feature important for staying safe and making well-informed choices when faced with potentially dangerous weather conditions.

Finally, GMRS radio is a great option for many different types of communication because of all the benefits it provides. General Mobile Radio Service (GMRS) radios provide dependable and affordable communication solutions, including increased range, reduced interference, adaptability, and interoperability. Everyone from company owners to outdoor enthusiasts may benefit from GMRS radios in terms of staying connected, informed, and safe during emergencies.

Chapter 2
GMRS Radio Licensing

Obtaining a GMRS License

To be able to regulate the frequencies used by the two-way radio (GMRS), the FCC mandates the possession of a GMRS radio license. In other words, an active license is required for consumers to use GMRS radios. Furthermore, with the most recent FCC changes in September 2017, any radio that can broadcast above 2 watts of power on the shared FRS/GMRS channels was reclassified as GMRS exclusively. As a result, GMRS radios can be either in-unit or portable.

Top GMRS License Requirements

The top GMRS license requirements are as follows:

- The applicant must be at least eighteen years old
- They cannot represent a foreign government
- They are only accessible to people
- The license covers you and your immediate family (spouse, children, siblings, grandparents, aunts, uncles) and requires no testing
- It only costs $35 and is valid for ten years.
- If you have previously been convicted of a crime, you will need to provide additional information about the circumstances behind the charges; however, this does not guarantee that your case will be dismissed.
- Finally, abide by the FCC's requirements and regulations

What are the FCC Rules?

For someone intending to get a GMRS license, you need to have these basic rules at the back of your mind;

- Upon request, a GMRS station, which includes handheld, mobile, base, and other parts, must be made available, along with any station records, to a licensed FCC official who asks for them.
- There can't be any sales pitches or ads for goods or services using the GMRS radio
- You can't communicate with Amateur Radio Service stations, illegal stations, or foreign stations using the GMRS radio
- You are not permitted to give misleading or false messages using the GMRS radio
- Do not pass any messages about anything that is against Federal, State, or local law using the GMRS radio

- No messages for public address systems
- No music, singing, sound effects, or other things meant to entertain
- There should be no ads or offers to buy or sell things.
- No ads for political candidates or campaigns
- No ads for political candidates or campaigns together

How Would You Apply?

This section demystifies the GMRS license procedure since the FCC website might be a little bit difficult and confusing. Here are the four simple procedures to apply for a GMRS license;

Register for a username and create an account:

Go to the FCC **Universal License System (ULS)** page and select New User Registration under the Filing subheading to register for an FCC username; you'll be directed to the FCC Registration Login page. Under the heading "**Need a Username**?", choose the Register option. This will direct you to the FRN registration form on the internet.

Further, you must check to make sure you are not already registered before completing the form. After putting your email address in the designated space, press the "**Check Availability**" button.

Proceed to the form if your username or email address isn't already there. Provide your name, address, and password in the form's fields. The FCC stipulates that the password must have a minimum of 12 characters, a maximum of 15 characters, and at least one lowercase, one uppercase, one numeric, and one punctuation mark or special character.

Choose a personal security question next, then type your response and hit Submit. There will be a procedure to verify your login and email address when the form is submitted. After your information has been confirmed and approved, click the **GoToCores** button to move on to step 2, where you must register for a FRN number.

Apply for a Federal Reserve Number:

Note: You can skip this step if you already have a FRN number.

You must have an FCC Registration Number (FRN), as the Commission refers to it, to apply for any kind of FCC license. You can be uniquely identified while making financial transactions with the FCC by using your 10-digit FRN. An FRN identifies you as a fee payer with the FCC, much as your social security number identifies you as a taxpayer with the IRS. You'll also need your SSN to fill out the form as well.

It's crucial to keep in mind that all licensing applications, modifications, renewals, and upgrades will require your FRN. Also, keep in mind that an FRN is your number for life once you get it.

To apply for an FRN, click the button that was stated at the ending part of step 1 or visit the FCC Universal License System (ULS) website. From there, navigate to the Filing subheading and enter your username and password to log in. You'll arrive at the User Home page using either approach.

At this point, you will see the following six options on this page:

Associate Username to FRN: Connect your username that you registered with an already-existing FRN.

Manage Existing FRNs/ FRN Financial/ Bills and Fees: Check & Pay Regulatory Fees, Application Fees, and Bills. You can also Check Red & Green light status.

Register New FRN: Fill out this form to obtain a new FRN, which includes a restricted-use FRN. • **Reset FRN Password**: You can change or reset your FRN password.

FRN Search: Look for FRN data that is available to the public.

Modify your profile: Make changes to your username profile.

Go to step 3 if you already have a FRN. The third option, Register New FRN, is the one that the rest of us should click on. This will lead to a box with radio buttons for settings related to registration.

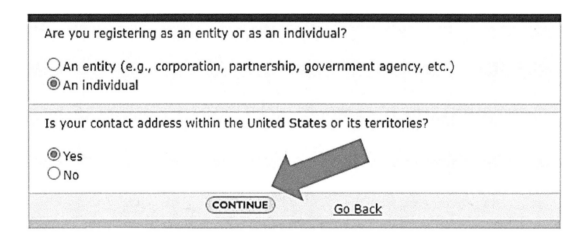

There are two categories of registration: individual and company. Since businesses are not permitted to apply for GMRS licenses, you would select an individual. This is the option to select since your contact address should be located in the United States or its territories. Press the **Continue** button.

Do you wish to proceed with a CORES FRN Registration or a Restricted Use FRN Registration?

◉ CORES FRN Registration
○ Restricted Use FRN Registration (Use only for filing Commercial/Non-Commercial Broadcast Ownership Reporting on FCC Form 323/323E in LMS)

CONTINUE   Go Back

This leads to another box with more radio buttons, select **CORES FRN Registration**, then hit the **Continue** button.

FRN Registration

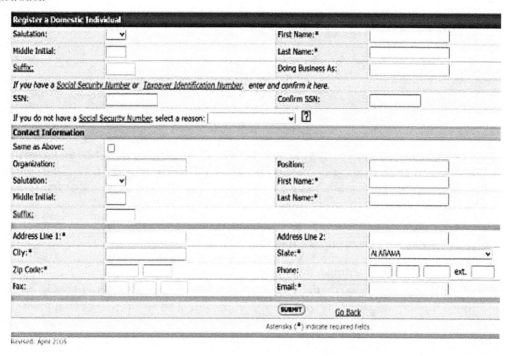

You may use this to be sent to the official FRN registration form on the web. Yes, an extra form. Fill out the form with your name and address. After the form has been completed and validated, you should be sent to a page with your FRN registration data and your assigned FRN number. This number should appear at the top of the information box. Considering how stressful it is to apply for this number, you should write it down and save it somewhere safe in case you need it later. Note that you have to connect your existing FRNs to your account before you manage them. To do this, go back to the User Home page, choose Associate Username to FRN, and fill out the short form.

Submit your licensing application

After obtaining your FRN, you may start the real application procedure for a license. Navigate to the **FCC Universal License System (ULS)** page and choose File Online under the Filing subheading. This ought to direct you to the login page for **License Manager**. To log in, enter your new FRN number and password.

Now you ought to be on the page for **My Licenses**. Select the "**Apply for a New License**" link located on the left sidebar. This will direct you to an additional page where you may choose the service license you wish to apply for, using a drop-down menu. Thereafter click on **General Mobile Radio (GMRS), option ZA**. After selecting No in each of the three drop-down menus on the following page, click the continue button once again to be directed to—**you guessed it**—another form. After completing it and submitting it, you ought to be sent to the **Manage Existing FRN(s) page**.

This page features four options that may be chosen from:

- Manage FRNs
- FRN Financial
- Regulatory Fee Manager
- ULS Pay Fees

You are not done yet; you still have to pay the fee. Although, this would be an easy-to-understand step at the end of an application process on a normal website. After completing the application and clicking "Pay," you're done. However, this isn't your typical website, the FCC is in charge of it. This implies that it must be overly difficult for some security reasons.

Make payment for the application fee:

To access the **Manage Existing FRN(s) page**, click on **FRN Financial**. This will take you to the page where the payment may be made. The option to **View/Make Payments** should be on the right, and your FRN number should be presented on the left. The FRN is mentioned under the heading **Awaiting Payment Confirmation**, and there's a **Make Payment option** to the right of that. Clicking the option will take you to an additional page.

Submit the payment form after filling it out and clicking the link. This concludes the procedure for you.

The FCC should provide your GMRS call sign in a few days. To see the status of your callsign and license, go into the ULS License Manager.

FCC Regulations and Compliance

The bulk of the regulations regarding GMRS is stipulated in a part of the **Title 47 of the Code of Federal Regulation also known as SUB PART E- GENERAL MOBILE RADIO SERVICE**, provided in **Section 95** of the said law. A rundown analysis of the aforementioned has been reproduced below;

Section 95.1701 Scope:

This section includes regulations that are specific to the General Mobile Radio Service (GMRS) and do not apply elsewhere.

Section 95.1703 provides definitions for GENERAL MOBILE RADIO SERVICE:

General Mobile Radio Service (GMRS): A mobile service that enables individuals and their families to communicate through voice and limited data applications. It is designed to assist licensees and their family members in various activities, such as providing voluntary help to the public in times of emergencies and natural disasters.

GMRS license that has been grandfathered: A non-individual entity, such as a partnership, corporation, association, or governmental unit, can hold a GMRS license if it has renewed a license issued before July 31, 1987.

Section 95.1705 Requirements for individual licenses, eligibility criteria,

authorized operators, and the possibility of cooperative use:

Generally, one must have a valid individual license in order to operate a GMRS station. An applicant must fulfill the prerequisites and follow the relevant guidelines and procedures described in this subpart and part 1 of this chapter in order to be granted an individual license. They also have to send in the necessary application and regulatory fees, as mentioned in this chapter's part 1, subpart G.

(a) Eligibility requirements: The following lists the prerequisites for each license type under the GMRS.

(1) An applicant must be at least eighteen years old and fulfill section 95.305 criteria in order to be granted a new individual GMRS license.

(2) It is simple for those who already have a license to amend their name or address by applying for a renewed or updated license.

(b) Individual license holder responsibility: The individual license holder must make sure that GMRS stations are operating correctly and in compliance with all applicable regulations in this section.

(c) People who are qualified to run a GMRS station: This section explains the requirements for people who have an individual license and are permitted to run a GMRS station.

(1) A valid individual license is required to operate a GMRS station, and anybody may do so.

(2) A person holding an individual license may delegate authority to members of their immediate family to run one or more GMRS stations. The spouse, kids, grandkids, stepchildren, parents, grandparents, stepparents, siblings, aunts, uncles, nieces, nephews, and in-laws are all considered members of the licensee's immediate family.

(3) In the event of an emergency, each individual license holder may designate another person to run their GMRS station and send a message.

(4) As stated in the following paragraphs, non-individual companies holding grandfathered GMRS licenses are allowed to provide permission to persons to operate their grandfathered GMRS station(s):

(i) Partnerships may choose to let their staff members and partners run their GMRS station(s).

(ii) A company may choose to authorize the operation of its GMRS station(s) by its officers, directors, members, and staff.

(iii) An association's GMRS station(s) may be operated by its workers and members.

(iv) A governmental entity is allowed to authorize its staff to run its GMRS station or stations.

(d) Individual licensees' responsibilities: A single license holder:

(1) As stated in this section's paragraph (c), the organization must specify who is permitted to operate its GMRS station(s), including family members.

(2) The organization may choose to limit who can use its GMRS repeater and reap the benefits of its operation, or it may allow everyone to use it.

(3) In order to comply with this section's requirements, the organization may prohibit some persons from utilizing its GMRS repeater.

(e) Term of individual license: Ten years will usually elapse from the date of award or renewal for every license in the GMRS. The methods described in this chapter's first section may be followed to renew these licenses. If there has been a regulation violation, the FCC may take into account a shorter licensing term when renewing the license.

(f) Cooperating with others to utilize GMRS stations: GMRS license holders may let other qualified parties use their stations, subject to the terms and restrictions mentioned in this section.

(1) The licensee, either alone or in conjunction with the participants, must be the owner of the GMRS station that will be shared. Additionally, the licensee may leave it alone or in conjunction with the participants.

(2) All stations covered by the license must remain within the licensee's control and access.

(3) The following circumstances must be met in order to share a station: There are three ways in which the sharing can take place: (i) without any fees; (ii) on a non-profit basis, where all participants equitably contribute to the capital and operating expenses, which include the cost of mobile stations and paging receivers; or (iii) on a reciprocal basis, where one licensee uses another licensee's stations in exchange for the use of one's stations, without any fees for capital or operating expenses.

(4) It is vital to guarantee that all sharing agreements are executed in compliance with a formal contract, which needs to be preserved as a component of the station documentation.

(g) Limitations on licenses granted on grandfathered GMRS: Permission to operate GMRS stations at specified locations, on specified channels, with regulated antenna height and transmitter power was provided to those having GMRS licenses issued before July 31, 1987. Grandfathered GMRS licenses let the license holders continue operating those specific stations as long as they adhere to the established parameters for frequencies, locations, antenna heights, and transmitting power. The FCC does not accept applications to assign, transfer, or amend grandfathered GMRS licenses (apart from administrative adjustments to update contact information).

Section 95.1723 Pertains to the inspection of GMRS stations:

If a person approved by the FCC wants to inspect a GMRS station, the operator must let them inspect the station and anything related to it;

(a) In this case, a GMRS station includes all of the equipment that is used with that station.

(b) As applicable, the following documents make up the station records:

(1) Please send me a copy of every answer you send to an FCC letter or notice of violation.

(2) Every authorization in writing that was asked for by the FCC.

(3) Any written understanding about how to share things that are in line with section 95.1705(f)(4) of this part.

Section 95.1731 Allowable uses of the GMRS:

A person who runs a GMRS station can use their station to talk on the phone with other GMRS stations and FRS units in plain language, for business or personal reasons.

(a) Communications in an emergency: Any GMRS channel can be used to talk to people in an emergency or to help visitors. GMRS station operators must always give priority to all emergency messages.

(b) One-way communication: GMRS station operators can transmit one-way communications for a variety of purposes. These actions encompass reaching out for assistance or sending urgent messages, notifying travelers about hazardous road conditions, or performing brief test transmissions.

(c) Travelers Assistance: GMRS station operators have the authority to transmit communications that can assist travelers in reaching their destination or obtaining necessary services.

(d) Digital Data: GMRS hand-held portable devices allow users to send brief text messages to a particular GMRS or FRS unit, as well as request and send digital data, including location information, from other GMRS or FRS units.

Section 95.1733 Limitations on GMRS applications:

(a) Besides the uses that are not allowed as stated in section 95.333 of this chapter, GMRS stations are prohibited from engaging in the following communications:

(1) Messages related to any activity that violates Federal, State, or local law

(2) Messages that are not true or are intended to deceive

(3) Messages that have hidden meanings or use coded language (the use of "10 codes" is allowed)

(4) Material that is meant to entertain or amuse, such as music, whistling, or sound effects

(5) Messages that advertise or promote the sale of goods or services

(6) Messages that endorse or support a political candidate or campaign (messages related to the campaign business are allowed)

(7) International distress signals, such as the term "Mayday" (apart from when used to call for assistance aboard a ship, airplane, or other moving vehicle that is in imminent danger)

(8) Communications sent via a GMRS station and received via a wireline control connection

(9) Communications (not emergency communications) to foreign, amateur radio service, or unapproved stations

(10) Continuous or uninterrupted transmissions, unless there is an urgent threat to life or property

(11) Texts meant for public announcement systems.

(12) Section 95.333's provisions are applicable. Nonetheless, in the event that the licensee is a corporation and so designated by the license, it may use its GMRS system to provide non-profit radio communication services to either its subsidiary or another parent company's subsidiary.

(b) GMRS stations are prohibited from being used for one-way communications, except for the specific instances outlined in section 95.1731(b). According to section 95.1731(d), initial transmissions for establishing two-way communications and data transmissions are not classified as one-way communications in this context.

Section 95.1741 Outlines the height limits for GMRS antennas:

GMRS station antennas are required to meet the regulations outlined in section 95.317 to ensure they do not pose any threats to air navigation. Refer to section 95.317 and review part 17 of the FCC's Rules for further details.

Section 95.1743 Operators of the GMRS who are under the age of 18:

According to section 95.343, minors, people under 18, are exempt from being held personally liable for any inappropriate use of a GMRS repeater or base station. Any inappropriate operation that occurs when a person under the age of eighteen is running the station is entirely the responsibility of the one who owns a minor's individual license.

Section 95.1745 Pertains to GMRS remote control:

Despite the prohibition stated in section 95.345, it is permissible to operate GMRS repeater, base, and fixed stations via remote control.

Section 95.1747 Pertains to the automatic control of GMRS:

Despite the rule stated in section 95.347, it is permissible to operate GMRS repeater stations using automatic control.

Section 95.1749 Pertains to the GMRS network connection:

Section 95.349 states that using a phone connection to operate a GMRS station is prohibited. On the other hand, as specified in section 95.1745, GMRS repeater, base, and stationary stations may be linked to the public switched network or other networks only for remote control operation.

Section 95.1751 Pertains to the identification of GMRS stations:

Every GMRS station is required to transmit its "FCC-assigned call sign" after transmissions and at regular intervals throughout transmissions unless otherwise specified in paragraph (c) of this section. You have the option to include a unit number after the "call sign" for identification purposes.

(a) In the following situations, the GMRS station call sign has to be transmitted:

(1) Following one transmission or many transmissions

(2) During a sequence of broadcasts that extend longer than fifteen minutes, every fifteen minutes, beginning after fifteen minutes.

(b) The "call sign" must be sent orally in English or by means of audible tone international Morse code telegraphy.

(c) If a GMRS repeater station exclusively retransmits communications from GMRS stations operating under the license it operates under, and if the GMRS stations being retransmitted are accurately recognized per the rules described in this section, then it is not required to send station identification.

Section 95.1761 pertains to the certification of GMRS transmitters:

(a) Certification is mandatory for all GMRS transmitters (those that function or are designed to function within the GMRS) as outlined in this subsection and part 2 of the aforementioned chapter.

(b) Equipment certification for the GMRS shall not be awarded to any form of GMRS transmitter failing to adhere to the pertinent regulations outlined in this subpart.

(c) Transmitters possessing a frequency capability not specified in section 95.1763 are ineligible for certification in the GMRS; exceptions are when the transmitter is certified for operation in a different radio service that grants authorization for the frequency and necessitates certification. If a GMRS transmitter is capable of functioning in an uncertified service, such as the Amateur Radio Service, it is not eligible for certification for use in the GMRS. Every GMRS transmitter must enclose all frequency-determining circuitry (including crystals) and program controls securely, preventing unauthorized access or tampering from the exterior.

(d) Effective December 27, 2017, the issuance of equipment authorization by the Commission for handheld portable unit transmitter types will be discontinued under both subpart B of this part (FRS) and this subpart (GMRS).

(e) As of December 27, 2017, the issuance of equipment authorization by the Commission for handheld portable units that satisfy the certification criteria outlined in subpart B of this part (FRS) will no longer be permitted under this subpart (GMRS).

Section 95.1763 Pertains to channels for GMRS:

There are 30 channels in the GMRS, broken down into 16 primary channels and 14 interstitial channels. GMRS stations are free to broadcast on any of the following channels.

(a) Main channels using 462 MHz: Only mobile, hand-held portable, repeater, base, and fixed stations are permitted to transmit on these eight channels. 462.5500, 462.5750, 462.6000, 462.6250, 462.6500, 462.6750, 462.7000, and 462.7250 MHz are the channel center frequencies.

(b) 462 MHz interstitial channels: Only mobile, hand-held portable and base station equipment are permitted to transmit on these seven channels. 462.5625, 462.5875, 462.6125, 462.6375, 462.6625, 462.6875, and 462.7125 MHz are the channel center frequencies.

(c) Primary channels using a frequency of 467 MHz: Only mobile, hand-held portable, control, and fixed stations are permitted to transmit on these eight channels. Except as provided in section 95.319(c), mobile, hand-held portable, and control stations are allowed to broadcast on these channels only for repeater station communication or short test transmissions. The frequencies of the channel center are 467.5500, 467.5750, 467.6000, 467.6250, 467.7000, and 467.7250 MHz.

(d) Interstitial channels using 467 MHz: These seven channels are only available for transmission on hand-held portable devices. The following frequencies correspond to the channel center: 467.6125, 467.6375, 467.6625, 467.6875, and 467.7125 MHz.

Section 95.1765 Pertains to the accuracy of GMRS frequencies:

During normal operation, all GMRS transmitter types must comply with the frequency accuracy specifications given in this section. Operators of GMRS stations must make sure that these regulations are strictly followed.

(a) Under normal operating circumstances, each GMRS transmitter's carrier frequency must remain within 5 parts-per-million (ppm) of the channel center frequencies specified in section 95.1763, while broadcasting an emission with an occupied bandwidth of more than 12.5 kHz.

(b) Under normal operating circumstances, each GMRS transmitter's carrier frequency must remain within 2.5 ppm of the channel center frequencies specified in section 95.1763, while broadcasting an emission with an occupied bandwidth of 12.5 kHz or less.

Section 95.1767 Outlines the limitation to the power for GMRS transmissions:

The transmitting power limitations for GMRS stations are listed here. The particular channels being used and the kind of station being used decide the maximum transmitting power.

(a) Primary channels using a 462/467 MHz frequency for operation: Stations that broadcast on the 462 MHz or 467 MHz main channels are subject to the limitations described in this paragraph. Each kind of GMRS transmitter has to be able to function within the allowed power range. GMRS license holders are accountable for making sure that their GMRS stations function within these parameters:

(1) Mobile, repeater, and base station output power must not exceed 50 Watts.

(2) For stationary stations, a maximum output power of 15 Watts is permitted.

(b) 462 MHz interstitial channels: It's crucial to remember that base stations, mobile devices, and handheld portables broadcasting on these channels cannot transmit with an ERP of more than 5 Watts.

(c) Interstitial channels at 467 MHz: It's crucial to remember that hand-held portable devices broadcasting on these channels shouldn't use an ERP greater than 0.5 watts. Every GMRS transmitter must be meticulously engineered to guarantee that the Effective Radiated Power (ERP) stays below 0.5 watts.

Section 95.1771 outlines the various types of GMRS emissions:

To comply with the emission capability requirements mentioned in this section, every kind of GMRS transmitter has to be properly built. Ensuring adherence to these laws is crucial while operating GMRS stations.

(a) The capacity to transmit "F3E or G3E" emissions is a must for all GMRS transmitter types.

(b) The GMRS allows the use of the following emission types: "A1D, F1D, G1D, H1D, J1D, R1D, A3E, F3E, G3E, H3E, J3E, R3E, F2D, and G2D". The equipment being approved under this subpart may transmit other emissions for use in other services. When the equipment is used in the GMRS, these emission sorts have to be able to be shut off.

Section 95 1.773 Relates to the permitted bandwidths for GMRS:

Every GMRS transmitter type must be meticulously engineered to guarantee that the occupied bandwidth stays within the permitted bounds for the channels being used. Ensuring that GMRS stations are operated in compliance with these regulations is crucial.

(a) Primary channels: GMRS transmitters operating on the 467 MHz main channels (see section 95.1763) or the 462 MHz main channels (see part 95.1763) are allowed to use a bandwidth of 20 kHz.

(b) Interstitial channels: GMRS transmitters are permitted to use a bandwidth of 20 kHz on the 462 MHz interstitial channels and 12.5 kHz on the 467 MHz interstitial channels.

(c) Digital data transmissions: Only the main channels and interstitial channels in the 462 MHz and 467 MHz bands are available for digital data communications.

Section 95.1775 Outlines the modulation requirements for GMRS:

Each kind of GMRS transmitter has to be carefully built to satisfy the specifications for modulation given in this section. It is necessary to make sure that GMRS stations are run in compliance with these specifications.

(a) Primary channels: Emissions on the primary channels may have a maximum frequency variation of ± 5 kHz.

(b) 462 MHz interstitial channels: A maximum frequency variation of ± 5 kHz is required for emissions to be broadcast on 462 MHz interstitial channels.

(c) 467 MHz interstitial channels: It's crucial to make sure that the peak frequency variation doesn't go over ± 2.5 kHz in order for emissions to be broadcast on these channels. Furthermore, it is important to remember that 3.125 kHz is the maximum audio frequency that should be contributing substantially to modulation.

(d) Overmodulation: All GMRS transmitters must have a system that prevents high audio levels from generating overmodulation, except for mobile station transmitters with a power output of 2.5 W or less.

(e) Audio filter: Unless it satisfies the criteria specified in section 95.1779 (without filtering), every kind of GMRS transmitter must include audio frequency low pass filtering;

(1) It is important to place the filter between the modulation limiter and the modulated stage of the transmitter.

(2) For each frequency (f in kHz) between 3 and 20 kHz, the filter must have an attenuation of at least 60 log (f/3) dB greater than the attenuation at 1 kHz. Attenuation at frequencies higher than 20 kHz must be at least 50 dB greater than attenuation at 1 kHz.

Section 95.1777 Pertains to GMRS tone transmissions:

GMRS transmitters can transmit various tones for different purposes. These tones are used for station identification, repeater station access, selective calling, receiver squelch activation, and the establishment or maintenance of connections with certain stations.

Section 95.1779 Outlines the limits for unwanted emissions in GMRS:

Each GMRS transmitter has to be carefully engineered to comply with the unwanted emissions limitations listed in this section.

(a) **Masks for emissions:** The table below lists the emission masks that apply to transmitting devices in the GMRS. The values in the attenuation requirements column line up with the numbers in the regulation paragraph under this section's paragraph (b);

Emission types filter	Attenuation requirements
A1D, A3E, F1D, G1D, F2D, F3E, G3E with audio filter	(1), (2), (7)
A1D, A3E, F1D, G1D, F3E, G3E without audio filter	(3), (4), (7)
H1D, J1D, R1D, H3E, J3E, R2E	(5), (6), (7)

(1) Section 95.1775(e) specifies the filtering requirement for GMRS transmitters.

(2) If the transmitter output power is measured in the same way, the measurement of undesired emission power may be performed using either mean power or peak envelope power.

(b) **Requirement for Attenuation**: Unwanted emissions shall be attenuated below the transmitter output power in "Watts (P)", and by at least;

(1) "25 dB (decibels)" on any frequency that is outside the authorized bandwidth center by more than 50% up to and including 100% of the authorized bandwidth;

(2) Any frequency that is beyond the approved bandwidth center by more than 100% up to and including 250% of the permissible bandwidth is subject to a 35 dB decrease.

(3) Any frequency that is moved by a displacement frequency "(fd in kHz) higher than 5 kHz" but not more than "10 kHz" from the center of the permissible bandwidth is subject to the logarithmic value of 83 times the ratio of "fd divided by 5", expressed in decibels.

(4) "50 + 10 log (P) dB or 116 log (fd ÷ 6.1) dB", whichever is lower, is used to calculate the attenuation. This covers all frequencies up to and including 250% of the approved bandwidth that is further than or equal to 10 kHz from the authorized bandwidth center.

(5) Any frequency that is beyond the permissible bandwidth center by more than 50% up to and including 150% of the authorized bandwidth is subject to a 25 dB decrease.

(6) On frequencies that are beyond the permissible bandwidth by more than 150% up to and including 250% of the authorized bandwidth, a "35 dB" drop is noted.

(7) Any frequency that is more than 250% distant from the center of the permissible bandwidth is represented by the equation, which computes the decibel value of "43 + 10" times the logarithm of P.

(c) **Measuring bandwidths:** Using a reference bandwidth of "300 Hz", the intensity of unwanted emissions within the frequency ranges described in this section's paragraphs (b)(1) through (4) is evaluated. A reference bandwidth of at least "30 kHz" is used to measure the intensity of unwanted emissions within the frequency range specified in this section's paragraph (b)(5).

(d) **Measurement conditions**: This section's specifications apply to all GMRS transmitter types, whether or whether they are equipped with approved add-ons such as an antenna, power cable, external speaker, or microphone.

Section 95.1787 Additional requirements for GMRS:

The rules specified in this section must be followed by every portable transmitter unit that is submitted for certification under this subpart.

(a) **Digital data transmissions**: The following specifications must be met by GMRS hand-held portable equipment in order to send digital data.

(1) Digital data transfers may deliver a brief text message to a particular GMRS or FRS unit, request location data from other GMRS or FRS units, or contain location data. Digital data transfers may be started automatically on a regular basis or manually by the operator. A GMRS device will automatically reply with its location when it gets an interrogation request.

(2) Digital data transfers must not take more than one second to complete.

(3) It is crucial to make sure that digital data transfers are limited to one transmission per thirty seconds and are not transmitted too often. It is important to remember, nevertheless, that a

GMRS unit has the ability to react automatically to many interrogation requests that are received in less than thirty seconds.

(4) The GMRS unit's antenna has to be fixed in place.

(5) The ability of GMRS devices to broadcast digital data on the 467 MHz primary channels is prohibited.

Section 95.1791 GMRS/FRS Prohibition of the sale of Combination radios:

From September 30, 2019, it will be illegal for anyone to make, bring into the country, sell, or offer for sale any radio technology that works under both this chapter's subparts (GMRS) and subparts B (FRS).

Responsibilities and Privileges of GMRS License Holders

Section 95 (SubPart E) of Title 47 of the Code of Federal Regulation also stipulates some of the responsibilities and privileges of GMRS holders. Thus **§ 95.1705, paragraph b of the said law** purports that a license holder shall have the responsibility to obey every part of the rules provided in this provision. However, on the privileges of holders, from **paragraphs c and d** of the above provision, the privileges of licensed holders may rightly be construed;

Privileges of License Holders:

Paragraph c establishes who is authorized to run a GMRS station under an individual license:

1. Anyone may run their own GMRS stations as long as they have a current individual license.

2. They can permit members of their immediate family to run their stations. Note; "Spouses, kids, grandkids, stepchildren, parents, grandparents, stepparents, siblings, aunts, uncles, nieces, nephews, and in-laws", are all considered immediate family members.

3. They can permit anybody to transmit an emergency message using their GMRS station in an emergency.

4. Non-individual entities with grandfathered GMRS licenses can allow certain individuals to operate their stations according to specific guidelines based on their organization type, such as partnerships, corporations, associations, or governmental units.

Further, **Paragraph d** outlines the duties of individual license holders which from the context of this paragraph can rightly be construed as privileges:

1. They must specify which individuals, including "family members", are authorized to operate their GMRS stations.

2. They have the option to permit anybody to benefit from the running of their GMRS repeater, or they can restrict its use to specific individuals.

3. They may prohibit specific individuals from using their GMRS repeater if necessary to fulfill their duties in this section.

Chapter 3

GMRS Radio Equipment Overview

Types of GMRS Radios

Below is an on the types of GMRS Radio, discussing their functionalities, features, and popular models.

First, let us first discuss the categories of GMRS radios and the types under each category:

Handheld GMRS Radio

The picture above is an example of a model of the handheld GMRS radio Suitable for personal usage, outdoor activities, and on-the-go communication, handheld GMRS radios are compact, lightweight communication equipment. To meet the demands of diverse user bases, they usually provide a variety of features, designs, and prices. Here are some GMRS types under this category:

Standard Handheld Radios:

These radios are intended for non-professional users who want dependable, easy-to-use communication. They often include a basic feature set that includes adjustable volume, keypad lock, and channel scanning. Some examples of GMRS models in this category, with a reputation for dependability and simplicity of use, include the Motorola T600 H2O and the Midland GXT1000VP4.

Ruggedized and Outdoor Models:

The way these portable radios are built makes them resistant to collision, water, and dust in hard outdoor conditions. They are perfect for hiking, camping, and boating since they may be constructed with waterproof or weatherproof materials. Examples of this model that provide GMRS connectivity together with GPS navigation and weather notifications are the Cobra ACXT645 and the Garmin Rino 755t.

Advanced Feature Radios:

Handheld radios have extra features including vibration warnings, in-built flashlights, and NOAA weather notifications. Group Call is a feature of some models that lets users talk to certain groups inside their channels. The Midland MXT400 MicroMobile, which has a small form and a high power output for installation in vehicles, and the BTECH GMRS-V1, which has dual-band capabilities and customizable privacy codes, are two examples of this kind of radio.

Mobile GMRS Radio

Above is an example of a model of the Mobile GMRS radio. Compared to handheld devices, mobile GMRS radios have a longer communication range and a greater power output since they are meant to be installed in cars. They provide characteristics appropriate for demands in mobile communication. Below are some types of GMRS radio under this category:

Mobile Compact Units:

These radios are designed to be installed in compact vehicles, such as automobiles, trucks, and ATVs. They usually have medium to high power output, which enables dependable long-distance transmission. Two such devices, the Uniden PRO510XL, and the Midland MXT115, are renowned for their small size and simplicity of installation.

Models with High Power:

Higher power output mobile radios, ideal for users in distant locations or needing an increased communication range. Also, external antennas may be included for better signal transmission and reception. The Midland MXT275 and the Retevis RT97 are two examples of radios under here; they both have a power output of up to 40 watts and may be used with repeater systems to provide more coverage.

Radios with Advanced Connectivity:

These are portable devices with a built-in smartphone or Bluetooth connection for improved functionality and hands-free use. Remote programming, voice activation, and GPS tracking are available on some models within this category; the Midland MXT500 MicroMobile, which has Bluetooth connection for controlling smartphone apps, and the AnyTone AT-778UV, which has dual-band VHF/UHF operation and APRS features, are two examples.

Base Station GMRS Radios

This is an example of a model of a Base Station GMRS

Base station GMRS radios are permanent equipment designed to be used in fixed places such as businesses or residences. They allow dependable communication over a larger range and often come with cutting-edge capabilities for unique configurations. Here are some examples of radios within this category;

Base stations equipped with repeater functions:

By connecting to extra antennas, users may increase the communication range of these devices thanks to their repeater feature. They are often utilized to create wide-area communication networks by companies, neighborhoods, and emergency services. Two examples are the Wouxun KG-805G, which has cross-band repeater capabilities and dual-band functionality, and the BTech GMRS-50X1, which has a 50-watt power output and repeater operation.

Programmable and Multi-Channel Radios:

Base stations with configurable capabilities and many channels for effective communication management and customizable installations. Channel scanning, priority channel selection, and CTCSS/DCS privacy codes are among the functions they can provide. Some examples include the QYT KT-8900D, which has up to 200 configurable channels and dual-band operation, and the Midland MXT400, which has 15 GMRS channels with NOAA weather alerts.

High-Tech Radios with User Interfaces:

Base station devices with huge screens, simple controls, and cutting-edge user interface to improve usability and functionality. They could include voice prompts for hands-free operation, programmable channel names, and touchscreen displays. Two such devices are the Yaesu FTM-400XDR, which has an APRS/GPS feature and a color touchscreen display, and the TYT TH-9000D, which has a backlit LCD and several programmable function buttons.

GMRS Repeaters

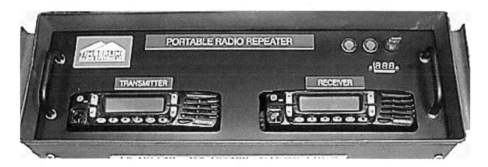

The above is an example of a model of a GMRS repeater

Specialized radios called GMRS repeaters are put in high places to increase the range of GMRS transmissions. They are essential for getting over difficulties caused by the topography and enhancing coverage in isolated or rural locations. Here are some radios you will find in this category;

Analog Repeaters:

These repeaters use analog modulation techniques and conventional GMRS frequencies. Further, broad-spectrum coverage is the standard feature, and corporations, law enforcement, and amateur radio operators often use it. Two well-known examples of devices are the Kenwood TKR-850 and the Motorola MTR2000.

Digital Repeaters:

These are repeaters with improved audio quality, data capability, and sophisticated features that are compatible with digital GMRS modes. Also, digital voice modes like DMR (Digital Mobile Radio) and NXDN (Next Generation Digital Narrowband) are supported by them. Examples of devices that provide easy integration with digital radio systems and network connection possibilities are the Hytera RD982 and the Simoco SRM9000.

Repeaters with Internet Access:

They are equipped with internet access for network integration, remote control, and monitoring. They also have IP linking capabilities, which let users link many repeaters together online to build networks for wide-area communication. Examples of models under this category are the BridgeCom Systems BC-GRMS, which has integrated web-based management software and real-time status monitoring, and the Yaesu DR-2X, which provides WIRES-X network connection for expanded communication coverage.

Below are further cited examples of models of GMRS, alongside their specifications within the aforementioned categories;

Handheld GMRS Radios:

Midland GXT1000VP4: Here are some of its features and specifications

- A total of 142 privacy codes on 50 GMRS channels.
- NOAA weather notifications that search for weather channels automatically.
- In open spaces, it can range up to 36-mile
- JIS4 waterproof grade to guard against water splashing or light rain.
- Functions include SOS siren, whisper mode, and group call.
- Rechargeable battery packs and two desktop chargers are included.

The Motorola T600 H2O: Below are some of its key features and specifications

- 11 weather channels and 22 channels with 121 privacy codes.
- IP67 waterproof certification, good for 30 minutes in water up to 1 meter deep.
- Has a water-activated flashlight that floats on water.
- Rechargeable battery pack or three AA batteries for dual power.
- Integrated VOX for hands-free use.
- 35 miles at best range under ideal circumstances.

Cobra ACXT645: Below are some of its specifications and features

- NOAA weather alerts and 121 privacy codes on 22 channels.
- IPX4 water-resistant design to guard against water splashes.
- VibraAlert vibrates to alert you to incoming broadcasts.
- Inbuilt SOS-equipped LED flashlight.
- Micro-USB charging cord and rechargeable NiMH battery packs are included.
- 35 miles at best range under ideal circumstances.

The Garmin Rino 755t: Below are some of its key specifications

- A 5-watt GMRS radio that supports 2-way text messaging and FRS.
- A 3-inch touchscreen with GPS navigation and preloaded TOPO maps.
- Dual GPS/GLONASS positioning equipped with a 3-axis compass and barometric altimeter.
- Automatic routing capabilities and NOAA weather warnings.
- Bluetooth connection for data exchange and digital communication.
- Up to 20 kilometers in range via GMRS channels.

BTECH GMRS-V1: Below are some of its specifications

- Handheld dual-band radio with amateur VHF/UHF and GMRS bands.
- 128 channels that can be programmed and have privacy codes customized.
- The scanning modes and hands-free operation of the VOX feature.
- An LED lamp and FM radio receiver.
- Robust construction and compact design.
- In open spaces, it has up to an eight-mile range.

Retevis RT76: Below are some of its key features

- A small portable radio with 121 privacy codes and 22 channels.
- Dustproof and waterproof IP67 grade for outdoor usage.
- Weather warnings from NOAA that automatically scan channels.
- Rechargeable battery or three AA batteries for dual power.
- For convenience, VOX and keypad locks are included.
- Under ideal circumstances, a range of up to thirty miles.

Mobile GMRS Radios:

With its many capabilities, these portable GMRS radios are ideal for a variety of outdoor sports, emergency preparation, and regular communication requirements. Here are some models and their specifications:

Midland MXT115: Below are the key specifications

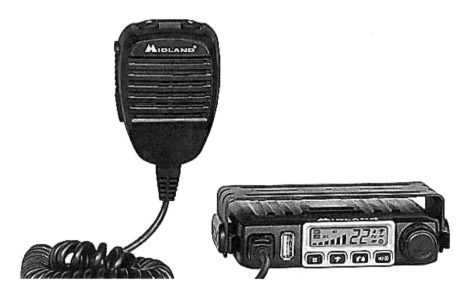

- A portable GMRS radio that can receive NOAA weather warnings and has 15 GMRS channels.
- A power output of 15 watts for a longer communication range.
- Keypad lock, channel scan, and silent operation.
- External magnetic mount antenna in a compact form.
- Interoperable with MicroMobile accessories from Midland.
- 50 miles at the best range.

Midland MXT275: Below are the key specifications

- A mobile GMRS radio equipped with NOAA weather warnings and 15 GMRS channels.
- An external magnetic mount antenna with a 15-watt power output.
- Comes with a keypad lock, quiet operation, and an adjustable squelch.
- A backlit LCD that includes a signal meter and channel scan.
- Compact design that can be installed in a car.
- 50 miles at best range in normal situations.

Uniden PRO520XL: Below are the key specifications

- 40-channel compact CB radio with quick emergency channel 9.
- An ANL switch and PA capabilities to cut down on noise.
- Channel selection, RF gain control, and squelch control.
- Front-facing speaker for output of high-quality audio.
- Compact design with choices for simple installation.
- Requires a different license in order to operate GMRS.

AT-778UV AnyTone: Below are the key specifications

- GMRS, VHF, and UHF bands are supported by a dual-band mobile radio.
- A power output of 25 watts and 200 customizable channels.
- Dual display with CTCSS/DCS settings and channel names in alphanumeric.
- Inbuilt flashlight and FM radio receiver.
- Front panel removable and remote mountable.
- In an open space, it can go for a range of up to thirty miles.

Retevis RT97: Below are the key specifications

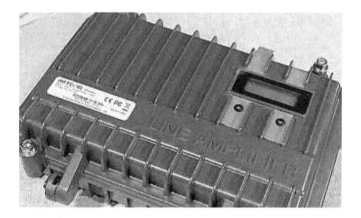

- A GMRS repeater that is portable and has a 10-watt power output.
- Small design with a tripod mount and built-in battery.
- Has a time-out timer and supports both simplex and duplex operations.
- An LCD screen showing the power and channel settings.
- Perfect for last-minute or emergency communication arrangements.
- Depending on the topography and antenna height, the range extension may reach up to 20 miles.

Midland MicroMobile MXT500: Below are the key specifications

- A small GMRS radio that can be controlled by a smartphone via Bluetooth communication.
- An external magnetic mount antenna with a 15-watt power output.
- A fully customized LCD with color names for each channel.
- Channel scan features and NOAA weather notifications.
- Interoperable with MicroMobile accessories from Midland.
- 50 miles at the best range.

Base Station GMRS Radios:

With a variety of features and power choices, these transportable GMRS radios provide dependable communication for automobiles, base stations, and transient settings. Below are some models under this category:

BTech GMRS-50X1: Below are the key specifications

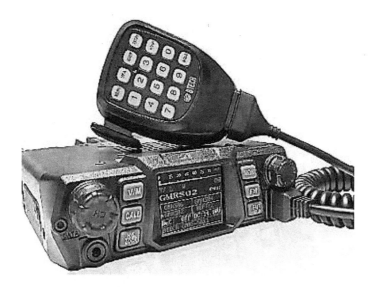

- Radio base station with 50 watts of power output and repeater capabilities.
- 128 configurable channels with privacy codes for CTCSS and DCS.
- Dual sync display for channel monitoring in real-time.
- Channel names may be changed and display choices with many colors.
- Easily installed with a removable front panel and an integrated cooling fan.
- Expand the range by setting up a repeater and an extra antenna.

Midland MXT400: Below are the key specifications

- 40 GMRS channels and NOAA weather notifications on a base station radio.
- A 40-watt power output for a greater range of communication.
- A backlit LCD that includes a signal meter and channel scan.
- Keypad lock, quiet operation, and adjustable squelch.
- Compact design that may be installed in a house or car.
- 65 miles at maximum range.

TYT TH-9000D: Below are the key specifications

- A dual-band base station radio with 200 customizable channels.
- An alphanumeric display that may be brightened or darkened.
- Voice prompt and tone scanning features in the CTCSS/DCS settings.
- A front-firing speaker that produces crisp sounds.
- Front panel that may be detached for installation by remote.
- It has a range of up to thirty miles.

Yaesu FTM-400XDR:

- A base station radio with digital modes and dual-band VHF/UHF operation.
- APRS/GPS capabilities and a 50-watt power output.
- A color touchscreen display that allows for arrangement customization.
- WIRES-X network link for wider reach of communications.
- Remote control options, Bluetooth connection, and voice instructions.
- 50 miles at the best range.

Wouxun KG-805G: Below are the key specifications

- A base station radio with cross-band repeater functionality and dual-band VHF/UHF operation.
- 999 channels that can be programmed using DTMF encoding and decoding.
- Inbuilt APRS and GPS receiver for reporting location in real-time.
- Customizable function keys, LCD, and spoken instructions.
- A front-firing speaker that produces crisp sounds.
- Can go for a range of up to 40 miles.

QYT KT-8900D: Below are some of the key specifications

- A base station radio with 200 configurable channels and dual-band VHF/UHF operation.
- An alphanumeric display using channel scanning and a backlight.
- Privacy codes for CTCSS/DCS that include voice prompts and tone scanning.
- A front-firing speaker that produces good sounds and has volume control.
- Compact design that may be installed in a house or car.
- Can go for a range of up to thirty miles.

GMRS Repeaters:

Advanced features and capabilities for amateur radio operations, emergency preparation, and wide-area communication networks are available with these base station GMRS radios. Below are some of the models:

MTR2000 from Motorola: Below are some of the key specifications

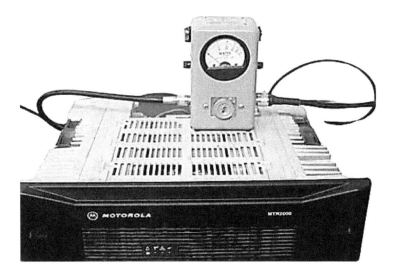

- A modularly designed analog repeater with adjustable features.
- A power output of up to 150 watts and a frequency range of 403-512 MHz or 136-174 MHz.
- Autonomously powered operation with continuous duty.
- Remote monitoring and built-in diagnostics features.
- Compliant with ASTRO digital operation and Motorola's MDC signaling.
- Expand the range by installing external antennas correctly.

Hytera RD982: Below are some of the key specifications

- A digital repeater that facilitates Tier II and Tier III DMR operations.
- A power output of up to 50 watts and a frequency range of 400–470 MHz or 136–174 MHz.
- IP Site Connect or trunked systems' IP networking capabilities.
- GPS location, remote diagnostics, and enhanced encryption.
- Dual-slot TDMA technology for effective use of available spectrum.
- Expanding the range via network integration and IP connection.

Yaesu DR-2X: Below are some of the specification

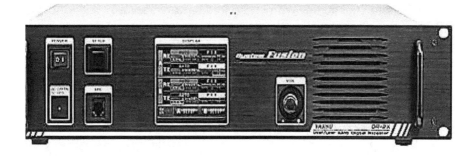

- Dual-mode digital and analog repeater connected to the WIRES-X network.
- A frequency range of either 420–450 MHz or 144–148 MHz with a power output of 50 watts.
- An integrated WIRES-X node for increased coverage that is internet-connected.
- Firmware upgradeable design and automatic mode selection.
- An LCD front panel and an easy-to-use programming interface.
- You can expand the range via repeater and network connection for WIRES-X.

BC-GRMS from BridgeCom Systems: Below are some of the key specifications

- A digital repeater with built-in web-based administration tools.

- A 40-watt power output with a 462-467 MHz frequency range.
- The ability to connect IP addresses for remote control and monitoring.
- Real-time status tracking supported by SNMP and email notifications.
- Allows for flexible communication using both analog and digital modalities.
- You can expand the range via network connection and IP connection.

Kenwood TKR-850: Below are some of the key specifications

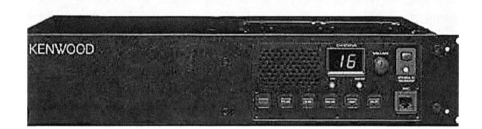

- Wideband-operating analog repeater with a modular architecture.
- A maximum power output of 50 watts and a frequency range of 450–470 MHz or 136–174 MHz.
- Front-panel LED indicators and an integrated cooling fan.
- Facilitates enhanced data and signaling capabilities.
- Constant-duty functioning with integrated battery backup.
- You can expand the range by installing external antennas correctly.

Simoco SRM9000: Below are some of the key specifications

- Digital repeater enabling DMR Tier II operation.
- A power output of up to 50 watts and a frequency range of 400–470 MHz or 136–174 MHz.

- Integrated IP networking capability for wide-area coverage.
- GPS locating, sophisticated encryption, and remote diagnostics.
- Dual-slot TDMA technology for effective use of available spectrum.
- You can expand the range via network integration and IP connection.

Things to Consider When Getting a GMRS Radio

Notwithstanding that, there are several categories of GMRS radios and different models under each category you can choose from. However, there are some basic things you must consider which would guide you when making your preference, for instance; What is the frequency range for GMRS? Is a professional license required to operate a GMRS radio? How can I apply for a GMRS license? Can a ham radio license permit me to transmit on GMRS frequencies? Is it possible to utilize a ham radio on GMRS frequencies? Which antenna is typically used for GMRS? What is the maximum distance that can be covered between two GMRS radios? What exactly is a GMRS repeater? How can I locate a GMRS repeater in my vicinity? More explanations have been provided below on these factors to be considered:

What is the frequency range for GMRS?

Below is an illustration of the frequency range;

Frequency	FRS Channel	FRS Power	FRS Bandwidth	GMRS Power	GMRS Bandwidth	Notes
462.5625 MHz	1	2 W	12.5 kHz	5 W	20 kHz	(1)(4)(5)
462.5875 MHz	2	2 W	12.5 kHz	5 W	20 kHz	(1)(4)(5)
462.6125 MHz	3	2 W	12.5 kHz	5 W	20 kHz	(1)(4)(5)
462.6375 MHz	4	2 W	12.5 kHz	5 W	20 kHz	(1)(4)(5)
462.6625 MHz	5	2 W	12.5 kHz	5 W	20 kHz	(1)(4)(5)
462.6875 MHz	6	2 W	12.5 kHz	5 W	20 kHz	(1)(4)(5)
462.7125 MHz	7	2 W	12.5 kHz	5 W	20 kHz	(1)(4)(5)
467.5625 MHz	8	0.5 W	12.5 kHz	0.5 W	12.5 kHz	(1)(4)(6)
467.5875 MHz	9	0.5 W	12.5 kHz	0.5 W	12.5 kHz	(1)(4)(6)
467.6125 MHz	10	0.5 W	12.5 kHz	0.5 W	12.5 kHz	(1)(4)(6)
467.6375 MHz	11	0.5 W	12.5 kHz	0.5 W	12.5 kHz	(1)(4)(6)
467.6625 MHz	12	0.5 W	12.5 kHz	0.5 W	12.5 kHz	(1)(4)(6)
467.6875 MHz	13	0.5 W	12.5 kHz	0.5 W	12.5 kHz	(1)(4)(6)
467.7125 MHz	14	0.5 W	12.5 kHz	0.5 W	12.5 kHz	(1)(4)(6)
462.5500 MHz	15	2 W	12.5 kHz	50 W	20 kHz	(2)(5)
462.5750 MHz	16	2 W	12.5 kHz	50 W	20 kHz	(2)(5)

462.6000 MHz	17	2 W	12.5 kHz	50 W	20 kHz	(2)(5)
462.6250 MHz	18	2 W	12.5 kHz	50 W	20 kHz	(2)(5)
462.6500 MHz	19	2 W	12.5 kHz	50 W	20 kHz	(2)(5)
462.6750 MHz	20	2 W	12.5 kHz	50 W	20 kHz	(2)(5)(7)
462.7000 MHz	21	2 W	12.5 kHz	50 W	20 kHz	(2)(5)
462.7250 MHz	22	2 W	12.5 kHz	50 W	20 kHz	(2)(5)
467.5500 MHz	N/A	N/A	N/A	50 W	20 kHz	(3)(5)
467.5750 MHz	N/A	N/A	N/A	50 W	20 kHz	(3)(5)
467.6000 MHz	N/A	N/A	N/A	50 W	20 kHz	(3)(5)
467.6250 MHz	N/A	N/A	N/A	50 W	20 kHz	(3)(5)
467.6500 MHz	N/A	N/A	N/A	50 W	20 kHz	(3)(5)
467.6750 MHz	N/A	N/A	N/A	50 W	20 kHz	(3)(5)
467.7000 MHz	N/A	N/A	N/A	50 W	20 kHz	(3)(5)
467.7250 MHz	N/A	N/A	N/A	50 W	20 kHz	(3)(5)

Note: certain lower-cost GMRS mobiles and portables may not meet the FCC's requirements for modulation bandwidth in GMRS. As a result, these devices may have weaker transmitter audio and a reduced range.

Is a professional license required to operate a GMRS radio?

Transmitting on GMRS channels in the U.S. requires obtaining a license and call sign from the FCC. However, it's worth noting that certain GMRS-compatible equipment is license-free in Canada. There is no need for a ham license and no test is required.

Generally, a payment of $70 to the FCC grants you the opportunity to utilize these unrestricted airwaves for 10 years. The FCC has recently announced a reduction in the cost of that license to $35. Currently, the price for 10 years is $70, but it will soon be reduced to $35 for the same duration.

Operating as a GMRS user, one can obtain a license and engage in legitimate commercial activities. One license can cover your entire immediate family. However, a company is no longer able to obtain a GMRS license.

Can a ham radio license permit me to transmit on GMRS frequencies?

Having a HAM license does not give someone the authority to transmit on GMRS frequencies, as the two licenses are not interchangeable.

Operating a GMRS station requires a valid individual license, as stated in FCC rules part 95.1705. Even if you already have a Ham license, it is necessary to apply for a GMRS license on the FCC's official website if you wish to transmit on GMRS frequencies.

Is it possible to use a ham radio on GMRS frequencies?

Only an FCC "Part 95E-approved" ham radio is capable of transmitting on GMRS frequencies. However, if it has Part 95E certification, it is referred to as a GMRS radio rather than a Ham radio. For example, the UV-5R is not suitable for transmitting on GMRS frequencies. Instead, the UV-5G would be the appropriate choice.

Which antenna is commonly used for GMRS?

You have the option to purchase a standardized GMRS antenna. GMRS radios usually require a BNC Male or UHF Male connector and should be pre-tuned and pre-cut. Simply install it and you're good to go.

Furthermore, operating as a GMRS user allows for the utilization of any UHF antenna due to its placement within the UHF band. However, it is necessary to adjust and optimize the antenna to match the GMRS frequencies.

What is the maximum distance that can be maintained between two GMRS radios?

Similar to a GMRS operator, the range of UHF radio services is typically limited to line-of-sight. To determine the distance to the radio horizon, one can make an estimate based on the height of the antenna. In theory, the distance between two hand-held units would be approximately one or two miles (about 1.5–3 km); mobile units, on the other hand, have higher antennas and can cover a range of around 5 miles (8 km). With a GMRS repeater and an elevated antenna, the effective range can be significantly expanded, covering a wide area of up to a 20-mile (32.2 km) radius around the repeater station. According to a source, the information provided is supported by evidence. Obstacles like hills and buildings can diminish the range. Operating at a higher power level doesn't always mean you'll get a direct boost in range. However, it can enhance the dependability of communication when you're pushing the limits of line-of-sight distance.

What exactly is a GMRS repeater?

A repeater is essentially a radio that can both receive and transmit simultaneously. Typically, they are equipped with powerful transmitters and large antennas. The repeater functions by receiving your signal and then rebroadcasting it over a larger area, effectively expanding your communication range.

Typically, the GMRS repeater is strategically positioned in a location with extensive coverage, like the summit of a towering mountain. Imagine being on one side of a mountain and trying to communicate with someone on the other side. It's frustrating when natural obstacles prevent you from talking to each other. If you have a repeater set up, it allows for communication between you and others by utilizing that repeater.

When it comes to Ham repeaters, the GMRS repeater is specifically designed to operate on GMRS frequencies exclusively. GMRS repeaters have a standardized configuration, while Ham radio offers operators more flexibility in configuring their systems.

Prior authorization from the repeater owner is required in order to utilize the repeater. Many of the repeaters in the United States are privately owned, often by GMRS radio clubs. However, there are also instances where individuals have constructed repeaters on their rooftops for personal use.

Operating on a GMRS repeater can be quite challenging, as it only permits one conversation at a time due to its limited capacity. It would be wise to avoid wasting resources when you are close and can easily communicate.

How can I locate a GMRS Repeater in my Area?

When operating a repeater, it is essential to have the correct frequency or GMRS channel and the corresponding CTCSS tone to successfully connect and activate the repeater. First, you'll need to obtain permission to use a repeater. Once you have the necessary information, program it into your GMRS radio;

- Reach out to your nearby GMRS clubs if you're familiar with them.

- Try searching on myGMRS.com. You can access a comprehensive list of the repeaters that have been registered within this community. There, you can find the necessary contact information if you require permission.

Accessories and Add-ons for Enhanced Performance

Below are some of the accessories that you might consider buying to use with the GMRS radio for optimized performance

Antennas

This is an example of an antenna that you can use for your GMRS radio

High-Gain Antennas: These antennas focus the signal in a certain direction to make the transmission range of GMRS radios longer. They come in some different styles, such as whip antennas and directed antennas like Yagi or log periodic antennas. Most of the time, these antennas have higher gain values than stock antennas. This means that signals can be sent and received better over longer distances. It's important to make sure that the high-gain antenna you choose works with GMRS radio bands for the best performance.

Magnetic Mount Antennas: Magnetic mount antennas can be attached to cars and help mobile GMRS radios receive and send signals better. The base of these antennas is magnetic, so they can stick to metal objects like car roofs or trunk lids. They come in a range of lengths and styles to fit a wide range of cars and mounting places. Magnetic mount antennas usually come with a coaxial wire that lets you move and connect them to the radio in a variety of ways. This lets users find the best place for the antenna to work best.

Power Sources:

External Power Supplies: These give constant power to base station GMRS radios, so they can keep working even during long contact sessions or power blackouts. It is the backup power supply's job to provide power in case the main power source goes out. It is very important to choose power sources that have the right voltage and current ratings for the radio's power needs to avoid damage or problems.

Packs of batteries and chargers: For mobile GMRS radios, battery packs, and chargers are necessary tools that let users extend the working time and charge batteries that are running low. Spare battery packs allow you to stay in touch while you're outdoors or in an emergency, and fast chargers let you quickly charge multiple battery packs at the same time. Solar chargers use solar energy to charge batteries in remote areas where there aren't any other power sources. This is a long-lasting and eco-friendly way to get power.

Microphones and Headsets:

Example of a microphone and headset for your GMRS Radio

Speaker Microphones: These let you talk clearly and operate without using your hands, even in noisy places where a portable radio might not be useful. For easy contact, these mics have speakers, microphones, and push-to-talk buttons built right in. As there are different user tastes and use cases, they come in different forms, such as collar, shoulder, and helmet-mounted types.

Headsets and Earpieces: Headsets and earpieces let people in secret operations or security roles talk quietly and reduce background noise. They make it possible to talk and listen to the radio without holding it, which is more comfortable and useful. Noise-canceling headphones block out background noise so you can talk even in noisy places. These items are great for police, security guards, and people in the workplace who need to communicate reliably and quietly.

Mounting Hardware:

Vehicle Mounting Kits: These kits safely connect mobile GMRS radios to cars, making it easy and safe to use communication gear while moving. Most of the time, these kits come with clamps, mounting plates, and other tools that can be used to place the items on dashboards, controls, or ceiling racks. They make sure the radio is fixed tightly and in the right place so it works well and is easy to use while you're on the go.

Desktop Stands and Mounts: These holders keep base station GMRS radios standing up on tables or shelves, making the controls and screens easier to reach and more stable. They come in different styles, like movable stands and wall mounts, so users can change how the radio is seen and where it is placed. These add-ons make it easy to store and use base station speakers, making them great for use at home or in the office.

Data and Connectivity:

Bluetooth Modules: Bluetooth modules let GMRS radios talk to supported devices like smartphones, tablets, or Bluetooth headsets wirelessly. They make it easier to use GMRS radio systems without using your hands for things like data sharing, remote control, and operation. Certain GMRS radio types that allow Bluetooth connection can work with Bluetooth modules. This gives users more options and makes contact easier.

Programming Software and Data Cables: Programming software and data connections let people connect GMRS radios to computers so that they can set secret codes, frequency channels, and other things. USB programming connections make it easier to move data between radios and computer software, which makes setting up and customizing the radios easier. Users can get to advanced functions and improve the performance of GMRS radio systems by using scripting software given by the maker or software from a third party.

Protective Gear:

Carrying Cases and Holsters: Handheld GMRS radios are kept safe from dust, water, and shocks while being moved and stored in carrying cases and holsters. They come in a range of shapes and sizes to fit different radio types and devices. Belt clips, bands, or loops on carrying cases let users securely connect them to clothes or gear, making it easy to carry their radios while they're on the go. There are extra pockets in some cases where you can put batteries, radios, and other tools.

Weatherproof Covers: These protect the GMRS radios and antennas on the base station from rain, snow, and other natural debris, so they can work reliably outside. These covers are made of strong materials like PVC or nylon, so they will protect you from the weather for a long time. They're made to fit certain radio and antenna types perfectly, and they have places for wires and plugs to go. Covers that are resistant to bad weather are necessary for base station radios that are put in places where they will be exposed to it.

Others include:

External Speakers: When there is a lot of background noise, external speakers make the sound output and sharpness of base station GMRS radios better. They hook up to the radio's outdoor speaker output and improve the sound quality so that you can communicate better. External speakers are small and come with clips that make them easy to place on shelves or walls. They work great in offices, workshops, and other indoor places where clear sound is important for discussion.

GPS Modules: GPS modules add GPS guidance and tracking features to small GMRS radios, making them more useful. They give people real-time information about where they are in emergencies and while they're outside, which makes it easier to find their way and talk to others. GPS units work with some GMRS radio types that allow GPS, so users can use features and services that depend on their position. They are especially helpful for people who like being outside, like walkers, and for first responders who need accurate and reliable guidance tools.

Chapter 4

Setting Up Your GMRS Radio System

The general idea behind using GMRS devices is the same, but the steps in setting it up can be different, depending on the brand and type. With that in mind, we will use the Midland GTX1000 as an example. Note, most of these steps can be used with other GMRS mobile radios as well.

If you already have a license, here's what you need to do to get started using your GMRS:

1. Put the battery in

The first thing you should do with a brand-new radio that you just took out of the box is put the battery in. It will give you power so you can use the radio.

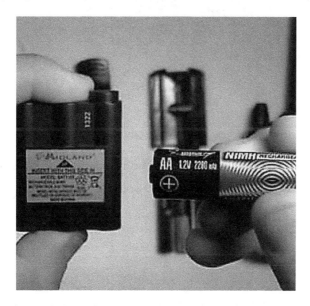

First, take off the belt clip and then the battery cover on a Midland GMRS radio to use it. You'll need to pull a latch on the cover.

Put in the new batteries while the cover is off the way. There are two kinds of batteries that you can use for this radio: four AA batteries or a NiMH battery pack. After putting in the battery, put the cover back on and then the belt clip back on.

2. Get the battery charged

The GMRS radio needs to be charged before it can be used. Of course, this only works if the battery can be charged again and again.

You have to charge the battery for 24 hours the first time you use it. When it's time to charge again, 12 hours will be plenty of time.

To find out when it's fully charged, look at the light. There you have it. You can now use your GMRS handheld radio.

3. On the radio

All you have to do to turn on the radio is turn on the switch. As you can see in the picture above, this one is on top of the radio.

This button, the ON switch, does two things: it turns the radio on and off and raises and lowers the volume.

Note:

- Turning it clockwise will turn on the radio right away. As long as you keep spinning, the volume will go up.
- The sound goes down when you turn it counterclockwise, and the radio turns off when you turn it all the way around.

4. Begin Transmission

Now that everything is set up, you can use your two-way radios to talk to each other. But before you do that, you need to set both radios to the same station and private code.

- Press the Menu button and then the up or down arrow to change the GMRS band or channel.

- Press again and again until you find the channel you want to join.
- To make sure you want to join the channel, click the PTT button on the side of the unit.
- If you want to talk, press the PTT button again and then speak. Don't forget to keep the radio two to three inches away from your mouth.
- The screen will show TX the whole time you're holding down the button. This means there is a transfer going on right now. When you're done, let go of the PTT button.
- Pay attention to what the other person says. The screen will now show RX, which means you are getting a signal.

However, you need to understand that communicating with another user via the GMRS radio is beyond pressing the PTT button. You need to learn the rules and etiquette of the GMRS, like how to talk slowly, show respect for other users, and so forth.

5. **Turning on and modifying the functions**

We've already talked about the general steps you need to take if you want to transmit using a GMRS radio. But GMRS has other features or settings that you can check out, some of which we'll quickly talk about below.

Locking the Keypad: You could hit the keypad by chance and change the programs when you're using GMRS for off-road contact or any other reason. The best way to stop this is to lock the keypad. To lock the keypad, click on the lock button; note for the Midland GTX1000, you will find this button in the top left corner. If you hold for three seconds, the passcode icon will show up on the screen to let you know that it is locked.

Making a direct call to someone: There may be a Direct Call feature on your radio, but it depends on the type and brand. With this, you can instantly connect to someone else without first sending them a transmission message. Press and hold the Call button, to do this. It's easy to call someone; just use the arrow keys to pick out their ID number.

Talking Hands-Free: During the communication, you don't have to keep your finger on the push-to-talk button. This is because, on GMRS, you can choose to use it hands-free. Click Menu until you see VOX on the screen to do this. To change the program, click the arrow keys. To move on to the next feature you want to create, click Menu again.

Setting up and installing an antenna

Installing and placing antennas correctly is a key part of making GMRS (General Mobile Radio Service) radio systems work better and cover more areas. When setting up and putting your antenna, here are some things to think about:

Knowing the Different Types of Antennas and Their Requirement

It is necessary to use UHF antennas with GMRS radios because they mostly work in the UHF (Ultra High Frequency) band. There are different kinds of these antennas, such as Yagi, Omni-directional, and Base station antennas, and each one is designed to meet the needs of different covering areas and operations. When choosing the right antenna type, you should think about things like gain, horizontal range, and the way the ground is shaped.

How Height Affects the Effectiveness of Your Antenna

Placing the antenna to a higher place makes its range and reception much better. Higher fixing places give you a clear line of sight and less signal interference, which makes conversation work better. It is very important to stay away from things that could get in the way of signal transmission, like trees, houses, and other structures. Attaching antennas securely to roofs or towers makes sure they are stable and won't be damaged by things like wind and bad weather.

Making Sure of Good Grounding

For protecting people and tools from electrical dangers, lightning hits, and static charges, proper grounding is very important. Follow the manufacturer's instructions for grounding the radio mast and coaxial wire to keep the equipment from breaking and to make sure it keeps working. Using a strong grounding system lowers the chance of signal confusion and makes the whole system more reliable.

How to Choose Coaxial Cable

The coaxial wire is the most important link between the receiver and the GMRS radio. It lets messages get sent with little loss. Choose high-quality coaxial wire with low loss to keep the purity of the signal over long transmission lengths. To keep the connection working well, keep wire lengths as short as possible to avoid signal loss. Also, use weatherproofing to keep the outside elements from damaging the cable links and stopping rust or signal loss.

Getting rid of interference

Electromagnetic radiation comes from things like power lines, electrical tools, and electronic gadgets, so antennas should be placed away from these things. Do a full analysis of the surroundings around the antenna to find possible sources of interference and then move the antenna as needed. Using the right blocking and screening systems can further reduce annoying messages, making sure that contact is clear and reliable.

What to Choose, Between Directional and Omnidirectional Antennas

Whether you choose a directional or an omnidirectional antenna depends on your communication needs and range goals. Directional antennas can focus signal transmission in a certain direction, which improves range and impact over long distances. Omni-directional antennas, on the other hand, cover all 360 degrees, which makes them perfect for situations where information needs to be spread widely within a small space. To find the best antenna setup for your GMRS radio system, you should think about how it will be used and how much range it needs

Changing the tilt of a Directional Antenna

To get the best signal receiving and broadcast from directional antennas, they need to be perfectly lined up and tilted. Try out different tilt angles to find the best mix between signal strength and covering area. By fine-tuning the tilt of the antenna, signal loss can be reduced and dead zones or signal dark spots in the coverage area can be kept to a minimum.

Carrying out Signal Tests

To make sure the antenna works and to see how well it covers the area, it needs to be put through rigorous signal testing. Test the signal from different spots within the service area to find places where the signal is weak or degrading. Write down the test results and use them to fine-tune where and how the antennas are set up for the best performance.

Antenna Rules and Regulations

Make sure you follow the rules for installing and placing antennas set by local laws, zoning ordinances, and related industry standards. Get all the permits and approvals you need before putting up radio equipment to avoid breaking the law and getting fined. Follow the rules about setbacks, height limits, and other things that the government says to make sure that you can legally and safely use your GMRS radio system.

How do I find the best antenna for my off-road GMRS radio?

Off-roaders who want to stay in touch on the roads can use the GMRS frequency band, which is between 462-467 MHz. Ideally, these antennas would be placed on a metal "ground plane" that is at least 1x1 feet, like the truck's roof. However, when you're off-roading, that's not always possible. You can put most GMRS antennas on bumpers, fenders, or spare tire hitches. Your next question might be, how to get past this? Without a ground plane, it's easy; just use an NGP antenna.

The **RFMAX RBC-450-5-NS** is the best antenna for GMRS radios when there is little to no need for a **metal ground plane**. It is a UHF whip antenna with an NMO base, so it doesn't need a metal ground plane. The antenna won't get broken in the wild because it has a **SPRING** base. It's also a "**base-coil**" style whip antenna with a collinear coil that will give you the best range.

To place your antenna, you can drill a hole in your bumper or fender and use a thru-hole mount. This would work well with a mount from our **RNMOV** part set, which you can see below. For this setup, you would need to drill a "**3/4"** hole. Most GMRS radios use a **BNC Male or UHF Male** jack/connector.

You don't have to make a hole if you want to use the **LBH3400** Bracket Mount. This bracket is screwed into the hood instead of a hole.

The magnetic NMO mount is another option for your antenna. You can attach it to a metal surface with a magnetic mount. Note; the RFMAX part number **RNMOM-195-SUM-B-12I-ST** is the standard recommendation. It has a no-scratch rubber mounting boot, a stainless steel pull tab, and a molded rubber strain relief to keep the cable from coming loose from the magnetic mount.

Installing an Antenna for GMRS Repeaters in your Family Farm, what do you need to do?

Every year, more and more family farms add GMRS repeaters to their radio communication systems to make the range of their two-way radios longer. GMRS repeater sales tend to go up in the winter when many family farms start their winter break and use the time to add the repeater systems to their farms.

Some things need to be thought about when installing antennas on family farms, such as choosing the right spot, making sure it is fixed, and even the right time to install it. Here are three things to watch out for when installing GMRS repeaters on family farms.

Weather Consideration

All outdoor activities should be avoided in the winter, especially during the snowstorm season in the north. Instead, outdoor antennas should be installed when it is sunny and calm, to protect people while the installation is going on and to make the antenna stronger afterward.

Choose a site

Family farms usually put the GMRS repeater on top of the house or on a relatively high piece of land that gets its power from the sun, like a hillside or a hilltop. In short, the antenna should be set up high enough within the allowed range to cover a large area and make calls as far away as possible on the two-way radios in the family farm.

GMRS Repeater Antenna Fixed Method

Family farms usually use two ways to attach the antenna: first, use straps to hold the antenna to the fixing tool, like a chimney; second, use screws to lock and fix the antenna on an attachment, like the eaves, the top of the signal tower, etc. For example, the Retevis RT97 GMRS repeater has two ways to attach the antenna. The original MR004 GMRS antenna has two ways to attach it. You can use the U-shaped clip in the first method.

It's also important to keep in mind that when the antenna bracket sticks out from the platform, its load-bearing and wind resistance should be looked at. If necessary, take some lifting precautions when installing the antenna bracket to keep it from warping over time.

In short, the antenna installation requirements will be changed by things like the family farm's terrain and the installation plan.

Power Sources and Battery Management

Power Sources

The GMRS radio can get power from the following sources:

Power from a Vehicle: GMRS radios often get their power from a vehicle's electrical system. This makes integration easier and allows them to keep working during mobile deployments.

External Batteries: Rechargeable lithium-ion packs and throwaway alkaline batteries are both types of external batteries that portable GMRS radios use. This gives users options when they are far away or in an emergency.

- **Lithium-Ion (Li-ion):** Rechargeable Li-ion batteries have a high energy density and a long run life. Because they are rechargeable and light, they are perfect for handheld GMRS radios.

- **Nickel-Metal Hydride (NiMH):** NiMH batteries are a good compromise between performance and price, making them a good choice for people who want portable batteries that can handle being overcharged.

- **Alkaline Batteries**: Disposable alkaline batteries are a useful way to power handheld GMRS radios because they give you power right away and don't need to be charged. However, they don't last long and are bad for the environment.

- **Lead-Acid Batteries**: These are usually found in base stations or backup power systems. They have a high capacity and are reliable, but they are too big to be used in portable settings.

Solar Power: In off-grid or rural areas, solar power can be used to charge batteries or power GMRS radio systems directly. This is environmentally friendly and doesn't depend on standard power sources.

AC Power: Fixed sites or base stations can be powered by AC mains electricity, which makes sure that they can work without interruption and communicate reliably.

Furthermore, since most GMRS devices run on batteries, most of them use replaceable batteries. However, some devices use AA or AAA batteries that can't be charged and are meant to be thrown away.

So, the batteries must last as long as possible. Two-way radios usually use nickel-cadmium (NiCd), nickel metal hydride (NiMH), lithium-ion (Li-ion), or lithium-ion polymer (Li-ion polymer) rechargeable batteries. NiCd batteries have a problem called the "memory effect," but lithium-ion (Li-ion) batteries don't have that problem. Li-ion batteries also have twice as much energy as NiMH batteries and weigh 33% less.

Also, there is the battery saver feature on the GMRS (although not found in most GMRS radios), which is called the low power mode or sleep mode. It helps the batteries last longer. If the radio is not being used for a certain amount of time, the feature automatically switches it to low-power mode to save power. The radio automatically switches to battery saver mode if there are no transmissions from it for more than 10 seconds. In some models of the two-way radio, this time can be changed.

Other Power Management Techniques;

- **Charging:** To get the most out of your rechargeable batteries' performance and lifespan, make sure you follow the manufacturer's instructions for charging them. Don't overcharge or discharge them past the suggested limits.

- **Battery Monitoring**: Check the battery levels often to make sure you can communicate without interruption. Built-in lights or alarms can let users know when the battery level is low.

- **Battery Rotation**: Set up a plan for rotating multiple batteries to spread out use fairly and keep each one from wearing out too quickly. This will keep the power flow steady and the batteries last longer overall.

- **Storage Considerations**: take the batteries out to keep them from leaking or corroding, and keep them in a cool, dry place out of direct sunlight to keep their performance and capacity.

- **Emergency Preparedness**: Make sure you have enough batteries on hand in case of an emergency or for operations that aren't connected to the power grid. Carry extra batteries or other power sources in case the power goes out unexpectedly to keep communication going.

Note:

Protect batteries from too high or too low of temperatures to keep their capacity and efficiency. Also, keep them away from moisture, dust, and physical damage, especially in outdoor or rough environments where GMRS radios may be used in rough conditions. This will extend the batteries' useful life and dependability.

Programming and Configuring Your GMRS Radio

In learning how to program your GMRS radio, we will discuss the steps and techniques using the RB23 GMRS radio as an example.

Get your software and cable ready to set up your RB23 GMRS radio

- You need to order the J9131P programming cable for the Ailunce HD1 DMR radio at https://www.retevis.com/usb-programming-cable-for-ailunce-hd1-dmr-radio.
- The software can be downloaded from the Retevis website at this link: https://www.retevis.com/rb23-waterproof-gmrs-handheld-5w-long-range-two-way-radios-us

- After that, install the software on your computer.

To program your RB23 radio, connect the cable to it

- First, connect the programming cord to the RB23 radio. Then, plug it into the USB port on your computer.
- Start the software and turn on your GMRS RB23 radio. You can try clicking the "Program-read data" button in the software.
- If it works, you should be able to join without any problems.
- If it didn't work, don't worry. Just make sure you installed the USB driver. If you didn't, you can get it from our website below the RB23 software.

Choose the feature for your RB23 programming software

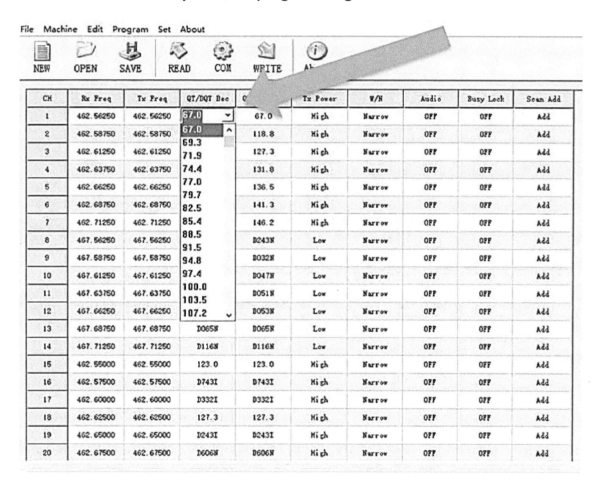

- The drop-down menu lets you change the **CTCSS/DCS** or turn it off. You can pick a different number or "**off**" here.

- You can also switch the power from high to low and the band from narrowband to broad.
- To set other features, click **Edit** and then choose **Option Features.**

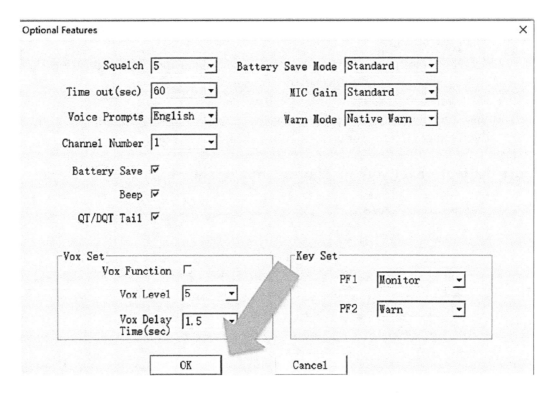

- You can pick the number you want, just like with the **squelch/TOT**.

VOX: To set it, you can check the box next to it and then associate a key with this function. For example, if you set **PF1** as the **VOX function**, you can press **PF1** to turn it on.

- When you're done, click "**Write data to radio**" and "**finish**." You are now done with the programming steps.

Programming with Chirp

However, alternatively, using Chirp is a widely known method for programming the radio.

CHIRP lets you work on a table of channel information that looks like a spreadsheet. You can list the label, frequency, offset, tone, and other information for each channel you want to use, along with the settings for different radio features. You can then "**upload**" this information to your radio at any time, and you can also save these settings in a data file that works with your radio (an "**image** file" with a ".**bin" extension**).

You can also "**export**" your channel settings to a file so that someone else can use them, and "**import**" a list of channel settings from a file. These files, which are in comma-separated value format and have a ".**csv**" extension, are not specific to any radio or model; they can be used with any radio. Here are the steps:

- Turn off your radio and plug in the programming wire. Make sure the connections are tightly in place.

- Turn on your radio; you might not hear the normal "**power-up**" message, but that's fine.

- "**Download**" the current radio picture ("**Radio**" -> "**Download from Radio**"). CHIRP will show a dialogue box that looks like the one in the image below:

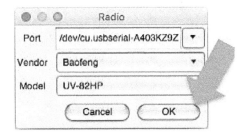

- Try finding the serial device that matches your programming cord, the radio manufacturer; and the radio type will appear in a pop-up window. Click "OK" to finish.

- Continue to follow the subsequent directions on your radio:

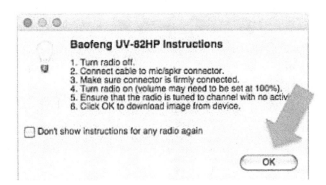

- Click "**OK**" to begin the download. A progress window should appear that looks like the illustration below:

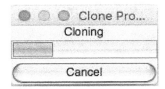

- You should now be able to see any radio stations that are factory default:

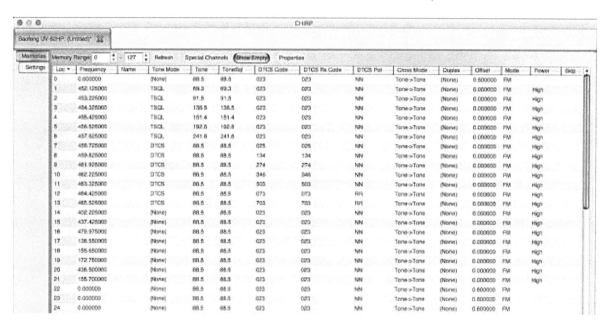

- Click "File" and then "Import" to bring in the "CERT Frequency List.csv" file.

- Choose "All" channels to import (CHIRP can also import a group of channels in this way:

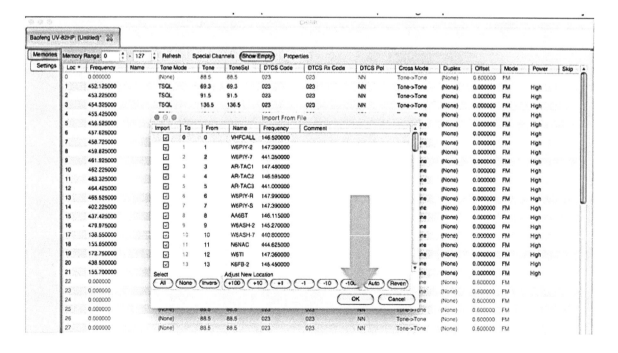

- Press OK

- In the CHIRP, you would be able to see all channels in your list of channels:

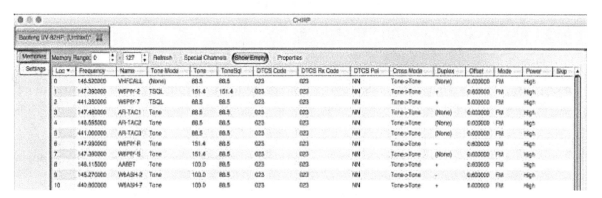

- -"**Upload**" the new shows to your radio (**"Radio**" -> "**Upload to Radio**"). Then, set up your radio by following the on-screen directions.

- **Click "OK**," and then follow the on-screen directions.

Further, you'll see a "**Cloning**" menu while the frequency list and settings are being sent to the radio. The radio may then restart itself. Turn off the radio, unplug the programming wire, and then turn it back on. Everything should be set up and ready to go.

You can **"File" -> "Save"** the whole setup you just uploaded to your radio as an "**image**" file with the extension "**.img**" if you want to. You can then open that image file with CHIRP at any time and pick up where you left off.

Chapter 5

GMRS Radio Operations

Basic Radio Etiquette and Procedures

Etiquette, or rules of behavior, have been set up over the years to make radio communication run more easily. People who use GMRS radios should know these simple rules and etiquette to get the most out of their time on the air: Below, the major rules and etiquettes of GMRS Radio communications have been provided;

- Unless otherwise permitted by a license, the English language remains the internationally recognized radio language.
- You can't talk and listen at the same time on a GMRS radio as you can on a phone.
- If you hear someone talking, don't talk over them. Just wait until they're done talking.
- Unless it's an emergency—if it is, let the other person know you have a pressing emergency message.
- Don't answer the call if you're not sure it's for you. Do not answer until you hear your call sign.
- Don't send any private, secret, business, military, or sensitive information. If you're not sure that your communication is encrypted at the right level for the amount of privacy. In other words, assume that other people can hear them.
- Make sure your radio is in good working condition by checking it:

    o Make sure the power is on and the battery is charged.

    o Make sure the sound is loud enough to hear calls.

    o Check your radio often to make sure everything is still in range and that you can receive messages.

- Write down the call signs and addresses of the radio stations and people you talk to often:

    o This is because when you talk on the radio, no one calls you by name. Each person has a unique call sign.

- Think about what you say:

    o Figure out what you want to say and who you want to say it to.

    o Be as brief, clear, and exact as you can in your talks.

- o   Don't use long, hard-to-understand words. Take your long message and split it up into several small ones.

- o   Don't use acronyms unless everyone in your group knows what they mean.

Four "Golden Rules" for GMRS Communication

1. Clarity: Make sure your voice is clear. Talk a little less quickly than usual. Keep your voice down; don't yell.

2. Keep it Simple: Make sure your message is easy for the people you want to hear it to understand.

3. Precise: You should be clear and to the point.

4. Safety: Don't send private information over the radio unless you are sure that the right safety measures are in place. Don't forget that airwaves are shared, and you don't have the frequency all to yourself.

Language Used in Radio Communication and their Meaning

- -   "Radio Check: This is used if you want to ask someone to see how strong your signal is. Or it can also mean Do you hear me?
- -   Go ahead: This means you are now ready to receive information.
- -   Stand-by: This means you notice the other person, but you can't answer right away.
- -   Ten Four or Roger: This means the message was received and understood.
- -   Negative: It means "No"
- -   Affirmative: "Yes" is what this word means. Note; positive words like "yup" and "nope" are hard to hear, so don't use them.
- -   Say It Again: What this means is to send your message again.
- -   Over: What this means is that you are done passing the message
- -   Out: What this means is that the communication is over, and now the channel is free for other people to use.
- -   "Break, Break, Break": This means you need to cut off the conversation because you have an emergency.
- -   Read You Out Loud and Clear: This is the reply you give when the other person says "Radio Check". Or it means your signal is strong.
- -   Come in: This means you want the other person to confirm that they heard you.
- -   Write: This means You know what was said.
- -   Wilco: What this implies is that you will comply with what the other person has just said.
- -   Repeat: This is used before you say something again.,
- -   Yes, that's right: this means Yes, sure.
- -   Take note: This means Did you hear me? Do you get it?

- Correction: This is said before someone corrects something that was already said.
- Do you read: What it means is Are you around? Please answer.
- Wait: This means Hold on a second. Or it means busy.
- Understood: This means I get it."

Phonetic Alphabet

On a GMRS radio, you will almost certainly need to use the sound script/phonetic alphabet to talk to each other. This is because many letters and words sound the same, that is why you should use the phonetic versions of letters that people often mix up, like "F" and "S," "T" and "C," or "M" and "N." This will help you make sure your message is understood. Here is a pictorial illustration:

A- ALPHA	H- HOTEL	O- OSCAR	V- VICTOR
B- BRAVO	I- INDIA	P- PAPA	W- WHISKEY
C- CHARLIE	J- JULIET	Q- QUEBEC	X- X-RAY
D- DELTA	K- KILO	R- ROMEO	Y- YANKEE
E- ECHO	L- LIMA	S- SIERRA	Z- ZULU
F- FOXTROT	M- MIKE	T- TANGO	
G- GOLF	N- NOVEMBER	U- UNIFORM	

Channel Selection and Frequency Management

Choosing the right GMRS (General Mobile Radio Service) channel and managing frequencies are important parts of making sure that transmission stays clear and efficient within the given band.

How to Understand GMRS Frequencies and Channels

The UHF (Ultra High Frequency) band is where GMRS works, especially between 462 and 467 MHz. The Federal Communications Commission (FCC) has set aside 22 channels in this frequency for GMRS use. Each channel has a capacity of 12.5 kHz. There are two groups of these channels: GMRS channels (8–14) that are only for you and common FRS channels (1–7, 15–22).

GMRS Simplex Channels and Frequencies

Channel	Frequency	Max Power	Bandwidth
1	462.5625	5W	25kHz*
2	462.5875	5W	25kHz*
3	462.6125	5W	25kHz*
4	462.6375	5W	25kHz*
5	462.6625	5W	25kHz*
6	462.6875	5W	25kHz*
7	462.7125	5W	25kHz*
8	467.5625	0.5W	12.5kHz
9	467.5875	0.5W	12.5kHz
10	467.6125	0.5W	12.5kHz
11	467.6375	0.5W	12.5kHz
12	467.6625	0.5W	12.5kHz
13	467.6875	0.5W	12.5kHz
14	467.7125	0.5W	12.5kHz
15	462.5500	50W	25kHz*
16	462.5750	50W	25kHz*
17	462.6000	50W	25kHz*
18	462.6250	50W	25kHz*
19	462.6500	50W	25kHz*
20	462.6750	50W	25kHz*
21	462.7000	50W	25kHz*
22	462.7250	50W	25kHz*

GMRS Repeater Channels and Frequencies

Channel	RX Frequency	TX Frequency	Max Power	Bandwidth
RPT15	462.5500	467.5500	50W	25kHz*
RPT16	462.5750	467.5750	50W	25kHz*
RPT17	462.6000	467.6000	50W	25kHz*
RPT18	462.6250	467.6250	50W	25kHz*
RPT19	462.6500	467.6500	50W	25kHz*
RPT20	462.6750	467.6750	50W	25kHz*
PRT21	462.7000	467.7000	50W	25kHz*
RPT22	462.7250	467.7250	50W	25kHz*

What you should consider when selecting a channel

- **Channel Occupancy Analysis**: Before choosing a channel, you should do a full analysis of channel occupancy to find any possible interference or overcrowding. GMRS radios have searching features that can be used to find active channels and pick a clear one for conversation.

- **Dynamic Channel Management**: Be proactive about channel management in places where communication is always changing, like cities or events with a lot of radio traffic. Always keep an eye on what's going on in the channel and quickly switch to a channel that's not being used to avoid confusion and keep the conversation clear.

- **Optimal Channel Spacing:** Making sure there is enough space between channels is important to avoid co-channel confusion and improve the efficiency of communication. You can improve connection and lower the risk of signal loss by carefully spacing channels and avoiding frequency conflict.

The Best Ways to Manage Frequencies

Coordinating and planning for frequencies: Coordinating how companies or groups use frequencies to avoid problems and get the most out of the band is an important part of effective frequency management. Make a detailed timing plan that takes into account things like the number of users, the service area, and the need for contact. You can make conversation easier and reduce conflict by giving people different routes based on where they are and what they need to do.

Adaptive Frequency Strategies: Keep your frequency selection options open and ready to change as the communication requires. You should be ready to change frequency when necessary to avoid interference or meet changing business needs. You can improve the efficiency and speed of communication in changing settings by using adaptable frequency techniques.

Geographic Channel Allocation: If you have multiple sites or a network that covers a large area, you might want to think about geographic channel allocation to get the best coverage and the least amount of disturbance. You can improve the dependability of communication and get the most out of the band by giving channels carefully based on location and operating boundaries.

How to Avoid Frequency Interference: Techniques

Squelch Control Optimization: On GMRS radios, fine-tuning squelch settings is necessary to block out background noise and weak signals, which makes communication clearer and reduces interference.

Antenna Placement and Optimization: Place the antennas in the best way possible so that they get the strongest signal and the least amount of disturbance from things like walls or electromagnetic sources. When placing antennas to get the best transmission performance, think about things like height, direction, and line-of-sight access.

Signal Boosting: Place signal boosters or repeaters in key places to improve signal strength and range in places where receiving is weak or there is interference. By carefully increasing signal power, you can make contact more reliable and get around service problems.

Frequency Scanning and Monitoring: Use frequency scanning to find channels that are busy or noisy and stay away from interference. You can improve the quality and dependability of transmission by keeping an eye on channel activity and band conditions.

Frequency management and Channel Selection Compliance and Regulatory Rules

Rules from the FCC Compliance: Make sure that all FCC rules about GMRS operation are strictly followed. These rules include channel usage, power limits, and licensing requirements. Learn the FCC's rules and guidelines so that you can keep your business legal and avoid fines from the government.

License Compliance: Make sure you have the right FCC license to run the GMRS and follow all of its rules. License holders are in charge of making sure that channels are used correctly and that rules are followed.

Channel/Frequency Maintenance and monitoring

Periodic Performance Evaluation: Keep an eye on channel activity and signal quality regularly to spot any problems with communication or interference. Do regular repair checks on your devices and tools to make sure they work well and are reliable.

Proactive Troubleshooting: Take quick action on problems you find through proactive troubleshooting and corrected action to keep the communication going without interruptions and reduce downtime. By making continuous upkeep and fixing a top priority, you can make the system more reliable and reduce the chance of problems.

Effective Communication Techniques

The GMRS radio can be used for many things, such as getting in touch with emergency services, talking to family and friends when you're not on the road, or talking to other people on your team at work. No matter why you want to use a GMRS radio, you need to learn some basic skills that will make sure you and the other person you're talking to during the call can communicate easily. Here are some techniques to keep in mind:

What to do before speaking

- Know who you are before you speak; learn callsigns and use yours before you speak

- Think about what you're going to say before you say it. Can you understand your words, and talk more with others?

- Before giving your team complicated radio instructions, try to think of the shortest, clearest way to say what you need to say.

Be clear and speak slowly

- Be aware of how loud you are speaking and be as clear as you can.

- Speak a little louder when you are outside or in a noisy place.

- People won't understand you if you talk too fast because they won't have time to process what you're saying.

- Remember that you tend to talk quickly when you are stressed, so take a deep breath before your call and be clear about what you want to say.

Note: You can spell your words using the phonetic alphabet if someone doesn't understand it or is confused by a homonym, such as way and weigh.

Be Simple and Precise

- Quit giving too much information or using long, hard-to-understand sentences.

- Instead of giving instructions all at once, break them up into simple messages that are easy to understand.

- If you need to talk about more than one thing at once, say the word "break," intermittently or after the end of each point. This gives the other person a chance to talk or ask questions.

- Use the word "over" when you're done so the other person knows they can talk or react.

- Say "out" to end the call.

Be sure that the person Whom You are Communicating with Understood

- Use the phrase "do you copy?" to figure out if someone got what you said.

- People won't always tell you when they don't understand what you're saying. Hence, they don't seem to understand what you want them to do, you should take the time to explain it again.

Do Not Interrupt

- If someone is talking, do not try to transmit something or cut them off.

- To make sure everyone understands, you should always wait until someone is done transmitting before replying.

Train your Staff Properly

- If you buy GMRS radios for your employees, you should take the time to teach them how to use them properly.

- Teach your employees the best ways to use radios, as well as radio terms and any business-specific radio codes. Teach them how to take care of and charge radios and how to use safety features like man down and emergency calls, as well as radio channels and zones.

Regular Radio Checks

- Make sure your radio's battery is charged and the power is on before going on duty

- Make sure the volume is high enough to hear calls

- Check your radio often to make sure everything is working and that you are still in range

Keep in Mind that Some Conversations might not be Private

- Don't send private or sensitive information—you may be using a shared channel

- Don't share private or sensitive information or talk about too personal things on the radio

- If secure calls and information are important to your business, make sure your radio has advanced over-the-air encryption

Chapter 6

GMRS Radio Range and Coverage

Understanding Radio Wave Propagation

Radio messages can go very far, but radio signals are changed by the channel they move through, and this can change how far the signals can travel and whether they are radio or RF signals. Different kinds of radio signals can move and spread all over the world. Some radio signals can only go over short distances.

For any radio transmission system, RF propagation is a very important matter. Radio waves will travel depending on a lot of things, and the radio frequency chosen will affect a lot of those things for the radio messaging system.

What does the term "radio propagation" mean?

Radio propagation is simply how radio waves move from one place to another, changing depending on the medium they pass through. One example is how radio waves move through different parts of the Earth's atmosphere.

Things that affect radio wave propagation

The way radio messages or waves spread is affected by a lot of different things. These are set by the medium the radio waves pass through and the different things that might be in their way. The amount and clarity of the information heard are determined by the features of the direction the radio waves will take.

Although, note that there may be reflection, distortion, and scattering. However, the final radio signal could also be a mix of several signs that have come together after going through different routes. These can add to or take away from each other, and the signals going through different lines may be delayed, which can change the shape of the final signal. Because of this, it is very important to know what the most likely radio transmission features are.

There is a wide range in the lengths that radio waves can travel. For some radio messaging tasks, a short-range may be all that's needed. In this case, a Wi-Fi connection might only need to be set up over a few meters. A short-wave broadcast station or a satellite link, on the other hand, would need the radio waves to go much farther. For example—the short wave in a broadcast station and the satellite link—the radio propagation characteristics would be very different. This is because the signals would have been affected in very different ways by the media they traveled through on their way to their final destinations.

Different types of radio propagation

There are several groups that different kinds of RF transmission can be put into. These have to do with how the medium the signals travel affects them.

Free space or Open Field Propagation

Here, the radio waves don't have to deal with other things that could change their path. They can move through space. It's only how far away you are from the source that changes how weak the signal gets. This kind of radio propagation happens when messages from the ground go up to the satellite and then back down again. It can happen with radio transmission systems, such as satellites. In the VHF and UHF bands, the most important way for short-range communication to spread is in an open area, where the signal received is a vector sum of a straight line-of-sight signal and a signal from the same source that is bounced off the ground.

Ground Wave Propagation

The ground or the land that waves move over changes them as they travel along the ground wave. They also tend to move with the curves of the Earth. These kinds of radio waves are used to send signals on the medium wave band during the day.

Note that ground wave transmission is only important at low frequencies, up to a few MHz, so we don't need to worry about it.

Ionospheric Propagation

Here, the radio waves are changed by the ionosphere, a region high in the earth's atmosphere. Systems that use radio waves to talk on the high frequency (HF) or short wave bands use this type of radio transmission. With this type of propagation, stations can be heard from other sides of the world, but it depends on a lot of things, like the radio bands used, the time of day, and more.

In the high-frequency bands between 3 and 30 MHz, the ionosphere is what makes long-distance transmission possible; although it depends on the time of day, season, location on Earth, and how many sunspots form on the sun every year. When very low-power receivers are used, they can talk over long distances. In this section, we mostly talk about VHF, UHF, and microwave bands that are above 40 MHz for short-range contact. At times, ionospheric reflection happens at the low end of this range. When this happens, sky wave propagation can cause signals from hundreds of kilometers away to interact. But for the most part, sky wave transmission doesn't change the short-range radio uses we're interested in.

Tropospheric or Sky Wave Propagation

In this case, the signs are affected by changes in the troposphere, which is just above the earth's surface. Radio waves at VHF and above can often be heard over long distances thanks to tropospheric propagation.

Sky waves travel because of reflections from the ionosphere, which is a layer of thin air above the earth's surface that is charged by sunshine (mainly UV radiation).

Along with these major groups, radio waves may also be affected in other, smaller ways. These might be thought of as sub-categories sometimes, or they might be very important on their own.

Below are some of the other types of radio propagation:

- **Sporadic E**: This type of propagation can be heard a lot on the VHF FM band, especially in the summer. It can make services less reliable because stations far away can be heard.

- **Meteor scatter communications**: Meteor scatter communications use the ionized trails that meteors leave behind as they hit the earth's atmosphere. For business purposes, it is the best way to send data over long distances (about 1500 km) when it is not needed right away. A lot of radio amateurs use it too, especially when there are meteor showers

- **Transequatorial propagation (TEP):** This type of propagation only happens under certain conditions and lets messages travel through the ionosphere when usual paths for that propagation would not be expected.

- **Near Vertical Incidence Skywave (NVIS):** Skywaves are sent out at a high angle with this type of transmission, and they come back to Earth pretty close. It gives you signals in hilly areas.

- **Auroral backscatter**: The Northern Lights (Aurora borealis) and the Southern Lights (Aurora Australis) are signs of activity on the sun that can mess up regular ionosphere propagation. Because it is hard to predict, this type of transmission isn't often used for business conversations and communications. However, radio amateurs often use it.

- **Moonbounce EME:** If the receivers have enough gain, you can hear faint echoes when high-power signals are sent toward the moon. Radio amateurs can talk to each other around the world at frequencies of 140 MHz and above using this method of transmission, which makes the Moon a big reflection satellite.

Also, there are RF propagation situations in a lot of short-range radio or wireless systems that don't fit nicely into these groups. One type of open space radio propagation that might be used in Wi-Fi systems is multi-refraction, diffraction, and reflection. However, this type of radio propagation will be greatly affected by diffraction, reflection, and multi-refraction. Even with these complexities, it is still possible to make rough models and guides for these radio transmission situations.

Factors Affecting Range and Coverage

Signal type, receiver, barriers, and signal power (wattage) are the main things that affect range. There is nothing that will magically make your coverage range longer. But together, they can make the difference between a range of half a mile and six miles or more. Let's talk about each of these.

Type of Signal

Radio waves are not all the same, to begin with. How they move and what they do when they come across things are different.

Since frequencies below 2MHz (Megahertz) are bounced off of the atmosphere, they can follow the curve of the Earth. Radios that are below the horizon can sometimes pick up these low-frequency messages from hundreds of miles away. **A general rule is that a lower frequency can move farther**. **HF radios, like CBs and some HAM radios, work in the 29–54MHz** range, which makes them good for some of these things. However, low frequencies can have other problems.

However, most GMRS radios on the market today work between 130MHz and 900MHz, but not CB or Ham radios. **VHF (Very High Frequency 130–174MHz)** and **UHF (Ultra High Frequency 400–520MHz)** are the two frequency bands that two-way radios use most often. Higher frequencies of radio waves move in straight lines (called "line-of-sight" signals) and **usually can't go beyond the horizon**; this is different from frequencies below **2MHz.** So, the farthest these two-way radios can communicate is as far as the sky, without the help of extra gear to "**boost**" the signal. But this isn't the end; there are more things we need to talk about in the follow up section.

Which is Better: VHF or UHF?

VHF (Very High Frequency) and UHF (Ultra High Frequency) are the two frequency groups (also called "frequency bands") that most GMRS radios use. People often ask, "Is VHF or UHF better?" The answer is that neither is better in and of itself; they both have their good points and bad points.

VHF waves are better at getting through things than UHF waves. VHF can also go farther. Also, if there were no obstacles between a VHF and a UHF wave, the VHF wave would go almost twice as far.

VHF can go farther and get through hurdles better, but that doesn't always make it the better choice. You ask, "Why?" There is a difference between how VHF and UHF waves behave around buildings. Remember that UHF signals are shorter than VHF signals; this is important to keep in mind when you're in or near a building.

For example, let's say you want to talk to someone on the other side of a company building. A metal wall with a three-foot hole is in the middle. Metal is not a good medium for radio waves. The VHF wavelength is about five feet wide and the UHF wavelength is about one and a half feet wide. The UHF signal can easily go through the door (1 1/2 ft). The VHF signal, on the other hand, is mirrored because it is bigger than the door. You can see that UHF is better at getting where it needs to go through smaller areas inside a house. Thus, the metal inside the building often blocks VHF waves.

However, as a general rule, VHF is better if you plan to use the radio outdoors where you will have a clear line of sight, this is because the signal will move farther. But if you're going to be using your radio inside or near buildings, in cities, or heavily wooded areas, UHF is a better choice because its signal will get through buildings better and won't get stopped as easily as VHF.

Antennas

Focusing on your antenna is one of the easier ways to make your range farther. There was one important thing that was not added in the preceding section when we said "the distance to the horizon is the maximum communication range"- which is the **antenna.** The height of your antenna is used to figure out how far away something is. That is, the exact distance to the sky changes based on how high your antenna is. If you want to figure out how far away the horizon is from your height, let's stick to **a simple rule of thumb: a broadcast with a 6-foot-tall antenna at both ends (send and receive) will have a range of up to 6 miles**.

Hence, the rule of thumb says that two people about 6 feet tall using a 5-watt mobile GMRS radio on flat ground with no hurdles will be able to talk for up to 6 miles. The question remains, are you sure you'll get 6 miles? No. You might only get 4 miles or even less. How can you make it feel more like 6 miles instead of 4? The answer is to get a better receiver or antenna.

Handheld Antennas

The Antennas of some Handheld GMRS radios are different. There are two main types of antennas for handheld radios: short and whip. A lot of GMRS radios on the market today have short antennas so that you can carry them in your pocket or bag. But short antennas can cut your range by up to 30% compared to whip antennas. So, if the range is important to you, look for a radio that has a whip antenna or at least one that lets you switch out the short antenna for a whip antenna.

Car, Boat, and other Antennas

Antennas on cars are usually attached to the trunk or roof, and they can stick out a few feet above the car. Because of this, cell radios can usually talk to each other within 10 to 30 miles. There are antennas on boats that work a lot like cell phones. Marine radios are very useful, except when they're out at sea, where there are no obstructions. The best place to use aviation radios is in the air, where there are no barriers and you are already very high up. The roof of a house is where base station antennas are kept, and mountain tops or very tall towers are where commercial broadcast antennas are kept.

A 25-watt marine radio, for instance, can communicate to antennas on tall ships up to 60 nautical miles (111 km) away. But, at sea level, that same radio can only communicate to antennas on small boats 5 nautical miles (9 km) away. The only difference between the ships is the mast height. Both have a 25-watt radio, or it may even be better from above. Note; a lot of airband radios have a range of about 200 miles and are 5 to 8 watts. See how the height of the antenna can change things? If you want to improve your range, raising your antenna is a better option than boosting your power.

Lastly, the range of your signal gets longer as you raise your antenna. When mounting an antenna, it's best to put it as high as you can. Also, don't place your antenna at an angle; put it up straight. For handheld radios, get a whip antenna instead of a short antenna to get the best range.

Obstructions

Most times, solid objects can sometimes block radio waves, that is why you need to keep in mind that if you want to communicate on the radio, metal is not your friend, because most radio waves won't be able to get through it. A typical practical example is this; Have you ever thought about why microwaves can't go through the glass door? Have you seen that the glass door has a metal plate that has very small holes in it? Microwaves have very short sound waves that travel at very high frequencies. Microwaves are small, but they are still bigger than the metal mesh's tiny holes. The microwaves can't go outside the oven because of the metal mesh.

Hills are other factors to consider. If you live near hills, they'll block out radio signals like metal. However, radio waves can pass through many things that aren't metal, like walls, concrete, people, furniture, and more. But the strength of a radio signal weakens every time it goes through something. Also, things that are densely packed together weaken the signal more. Hence, the range of a signal gets shorter as it goes through more objects.

Wattage (Power)

Handheld Radios

The signal strength is another important thing that determines how far a radio can communicate. The stronger the signal, the better it can handle getting weaker as it goes through things. The radio's power level, which is measured in watts, has a lot to do with how strong the signal is. A lot of commercial radio stations send out signals at 50,000 or 100,000 watts, but a hand-held GMRS radio, on the other hand, needs between 1/2 and 5 watts. Whereas unlicensed radios like FRS radios are restricted to 1/2 watts of power, MURS are limited to 2 watts, CB 4 watts, and SSB radios are limited to 12 watts. Note; 5 watts is the most power that can be used on naval, aircraft, and approved land-based radios like LMR, Ham, and GRMS. But the FCC decides what the highest wattage can be for each type of radio. Also, hand-held radios have small batteries, so if you use batteries with a higher wattage, they won't last as long.

Mobile and Fixed Mount (Car, Boat, and other Radios)

Most mobile radios can send out signals of up to 100 watts. But when put in a car, they run on the fuel of the car, because their signal is stronger than a portable radio's, it is less affected by things in the way; their broadcast can still only go to the horizon, though. Having more watts but not a better antenna is like having a big tube with a small hole in it. So put your antenna on top of your car as high as you can. Keep in mind that the sky is farther away when your antenna is higher. That is, a longer range comes from having more watts and a better receiver.

Finally, a radio's signal gets stronger as the wattage goes up. A stronger signal can go through more barriers without losing its strength, which lets it move farther.

Average Range Guidelines *

Wattage	Flat Open Terrain (miles)	Suburban Locations (miles)	Urban Areas (miles)	Inside Buildings (floors)
FRS ½ watt	½ - 2	½ - 1½	¼ - ½	3 - 5
1 watt (UHF)	2 - 3	1 - 2	½ - 1¼	6 - 8
2 watts (UHF)	3 - 4	1½ - 2½	1 - 1½	15 - 20
2 watts (VHF)	3 - 5	1½ - 3	¾ - 1	9 - 11
4 watts (HF)	5 - 6	2½ - 4½	1 - 3	10 - 15
4 watts (UHF)	4 - 6	2½ - 4½	1½ - 3	25 - 30
5 watts (VHF)	4½ - 6	2 - 4	1½ - 2	10 - 15
12 watt CB SSB (HF)	8 - 15	5 - 8	3 - 5	---

The picture above shows statistics. Also, keep in mind that the type of antenna you choose has a big impact on range.

Tips to Increase your Range

- Launch the "Monitor" function on your radio to listen for weak signs if you are close to the end of your contact range and your signal is weak.

- Increasing your height is one of the best ways to get a wider range. If you are close to the edge of your range and your signal is weak, try moving to a higher spot. It might help to walk up a hill or just stand on something to get bigger. Remember that a few feet can make a big difference in how far you can shoot.

- If you have a radio that works with both FRS and GMRS, change to the GMRS stations. For FRS channels, the FCC only allows 1/2 watt of power. GMRS channels, on the other hand, can have up to 5 watts of power. Note; 8 to 14, are only for FRS channels. Also,15 to 22, are exclusively for GMRS channels, and channels 1 through 7 are both FRS and GMRS.

- Most VHF and UHF radios sold in stores have at least two power modes. Make sure that the high power mode is selected on your radio.

- Instead of a stubby antenna, use a whip antenna. Also, when you put your antenna on a car, make sure it is as high and straight as possible.

- Make sure your battery is charged up because when radios' batteries are low, the messages they send are weaker.

- If the range is very important, choose a cell phone radio. A mobile radio's range can be three to four times that of a hand-held radio.

- **Use a repeater**: When repeaters get messages, they "re-broadcast" them to a farther away location. Setting up a repeater, on the other hand, is more difficult. This is why you can also look for a rebroadcast service in your area. Most of the time, these services cost money every month. On the other hand, the good news is that a VHF or UHF radio will work just fine without a rebroadcast for most uses.

- **Use a signal booster**: These can help you extend your range farther away. A repeater gets the information from your radio and sends it again with more power. First responder groups often use repeaters to make their GMRS radio equipment work better. Signal repeaters should be put in a tall building or tower to get the most out of them.

- **Make sure your batteries are strong**: Radio signals can weaken if your batteries are weak. Even though walkie-talkie batteries die slower than cell phone batteries because they don't need as much power, they do lose their power over time. Check your GMRS radio batteries often to make sure they are still good. A battery tester makes it easy to find out how much power is left in your walkie-talkie batteries.

Chapter 7

Emergency and Safety Considerations

Utilizing GMRS Radios in Emergency Situations

In an emergency, we might not be able to use our normal ways of communication. It's possible that the power is out or that we're not close enough to a cell phone tower to get in touch. Having a pair of GMRS radios is a great way to prepare for survival and will help you in any situation. Here are guidelines and things you must learn to prepare yourself for unforeseen situations:

- **Familiarization and Training**: Spend some time getting to know your GMRS radio and teaching others how to use it beforehand. Read the user instructions all the way through to make sure you understand all of its features, functions, and how to use them. Set up practice lessons to learn how to use the radio, such as how to make calls, change settings, and switch between stations. If you're familiar with something, you can be sure that it will work well when it means the most.

- **Channel Selection Strategy**: GMRS radios usually have more than one way to talk, and each one is meant to be used only for certain things. Before an emergency, do some research and make a list of all the channels that could be useful. This list should include channels that are set aside for emergency messages or government contacts. Make a plan for which channels to use based on the type of situation and the people involved to make sure contact is quick and clear.

- **Set Clear Communication Protocols**: Communication protocols are necessary to make sure that people can talk to each other in an emergency in a way that is both efficient and organized. Make clear rules about how to start and end conversations, such as who to call, what methods to use, and what information to send. Standardize how all users communicate to cut down on misunderstanding and make it easier to coordinate.

- **Battery Management and Backup Power**: Making sure there is enough backup power is important for keeping in touch during situations. Check your GMRS radio's battery level often and make sure the batteries are fully charged or changed as needed. If you want to keep your business running during long situations, you might want to buy extra batteries or portable chargers. Set up a plan for managing your batteries to save power and make sure that important messages get through first.

- **Optimizing the Performance of Your Antenna**: For GMRS radios, the best way to get the strongest signal and the longest range is to place the antenna correctly. Try different antenna orientations and heights to get the best signal receiving, especially in places where service is weak or there is interference. Adding external antennas or antenna extensions can make the signal even stronger, especially in places that are far away or have a lot of obstacles in the way. Check antennas for damage or wear regularly and repair them as needed to keep them working at their best.

- **The Rule of Listening Before Transmitting**: Follow the "listen before transmitting" rule to make sure the channel you choose is clear and not already being used for other conversations before you send a message. Watching what's going on in the channel lowers the chance of confusion and makes sure your message gets through quickly and clearly. Follow the rules for conversation and wait for the right time to send before you do so.

- **Clear and Brief Communication**: Being clear and brief is important for good communication, especially in an emergency. Make sure people can understand what you're saying by speaking properly and enunciating words. Use normal ways of talking to each other, like the sound script, to make things clearer and lower the chance of misunderstandings. Send texts that are short and to the point, getting important information across quickly.

- **Prioritize Message Content**: In an emergency, put messages first based on how important and urgent they are. Important messages, like calls for help or reports on safety situations, should be sent quickly and clearly. Avoid talk or conversations that aren't necessary because they could take attention away from important messages and make it harder to coordinate.

- **Use the weather alert features**: A lot of GMRS radios have built-in weather alert features that let users know when bad weather is coming to their area. Keep your radio on the weather stations and listen for tips from the right people. Keep up with changes in the weather and possible dangers, and make sure you're safe by adapting your plans and actions.

- **Collaborate with Authorities and Emergency Services**: When there is a big emergency, you should work together with local authorities, emergency services, or community response teams to make sure that everyone knows what's going on. Do what they say and give them the information they need to help with rescue and aid efforts. Set up clear lines of communication with emergency contacts or officials. This will make it easier to move quickly and effectively.

- **Maintain Situational Awareness**: Keep up with how things are changing by watching the news, listening to emergency alerts, and reading government reports. You can use your GMRS radio to get news, talk to other people, and plan what to do based on what's happening. Always be aware of what's going on around you and change how you react and what you do as things change.

SOS and Distress Signal Protocols

During an emergency, you need to know how to use the GMRS radio to call for help if you want to get help quickly and increase your chances of life. When you use a GMRS radio, these are the rules for sending SOS and emergency signals:

SOS Signal

Everyone knows that the SOS signal is an emergency call which means help is needed right away and that the situation is very important. Here's what you need to do to send an SOS signal through a GMRS radio:

-   **Choose the Appropriate Channel**: Pick a station that is meant for situations or that emergency workers usually listen to. Making sure you're on the right frequency is very important if you want your emergency call to be picked up.

-   **Send the SOS Signal**: Turn on the microphone and send the SOS signal, which is made up of three short beeps, three long beeps, and then three short beeps again **(... ---...)**. This design, called Morse code for SOS, is used all over the world to send an emergency alert.

-   **Send a voice message to follow up**: The SOS signal tells people how urgent the situation is, but sending more information through a voice message can help them understand what the problem is. Make sure to say exactly where you are, what the situation is, and if you have any accidents or medical issues that need instant care.

Distress Call Protocol

A distress call can be made using voice contact in addition to the SOS signal to give more information and show how important it is. If you want to make an emergency call on a GMRS radio, do these things:

-   **Choose an Emergency Channel**: Change to a channel that is marked for crisis calls or that is often used for emergency messages. This makes sure that the people who are most likely to help hear your emergency call.

-   **Say the Phrase "Mayday, Mayday, Mayday":** To start your emergency call, say "Mayday" three times all at once. This widely-known emergency call lets people know how bad things are and that you need help right away.

-   **Provide the necessary Information**: After calling "Mayday," you must give important information about your situation, such as where you are, what the problem is, how many people are involved, and if you need instant help. This knowledge helps first rescuers figure out what's going on and how to handle it.

- **Wait for Acknowledgement and Response**: Once you've sent out your crisis call, keep an eye on the emergency line to see if emergency services or other users have acknowledged it. Prepare to send your message again if needed, and do what the people who answer tell you to do.

Using Distress Signals When There Isn't an Emergency

SOS and other distress signals should only be used in real situations so as not to cause unnecessary worry or confusion. If you use these signs in the wrong way, they may not be as important and may cause delays in responding to real situations.

Confirmation and Coordination

After sending a distress signal, keep an eye on the emergency channel to see if emergency services or other local groups respond or acknowledge it. Give new information about your situation as needed, and do what the rescuers tell you to do. Working together with emergency services is very important for a quick and effective reaction.

Practice and Preparations

Learn how to use distress signals and practice using them before you need to in an emergency. You should make sure that everyone in your group or company who uses a GMRS radio knows how to send and receive emergency signs. Regular training and drills can help reinforce these rules and make people more ready for emergencies.

Safety Precautions and Best Practices

Although the GMRS radios are very useful during emergencies, they should only be used after carefully thinking about safety measures and best practices. Here are some best practices and safety steps for using GMRS radios to make sure you can communicate reliably and stay safe:

- **Thoroughly Read the User Manual**: The manufacturer's user manual is the best way to learn about your GMRS radio's features, functions, and how to use it. Before you use it, take the time to read the instructions carefully and get to know it. It's important to know how your radio works to communicate safely and effectively.

- **Regular Battery Maintenance**: The battery life of any electronic device is the most important thing to think about. Check your GMRS radio's battery level often to make sure it stays at the right amount of power. As needed, replace or charge the batteries to keep them from running out of power during important times. Regular battery repair makes sure that you can communicate without problems when you need to.

- **Handle with Care:** Be very careful with your GMRS radio so that it doesn't get broken or stop working. Do not drop or hit the gadget in a way that could damage it. Place the radio in a secure case when not in use to keep it from getting broken. Protect the antenna from breaking or bending as well, since damage to the antenna can make signal transfer much less effective.

- **Compliance with Regulations**: Make sure you follow the rules for using GMRS radios in your area. To make sure you're following the law, learn about frequency limits and license requirements. Following the rules not only keeps you out of trouble with the law, but it also encourages careful and polite use of radio channels.

- **Monitoring the Weather**: Pay close attention to the present and expected weather, especially when using GMRS radios outside. Storms, high winds, and extreme temperatures are all examples of severe weather that can be very dangerous. Watch out for bad weather and be ready to take cover or change your plans as needed to lower the risks that come with it.

- **Maintaining Situational Awareness:** When using GMRS radios, especially in remote or unknown areas, keep your situational awareness at a high level. Keep an eye on your surroundings and any possible dangers, such as rough ground, wild animals, or changing weather. Talking to your group or emergency contacts regularly helps everyone stay safe and aware.

- **Clear Communication Protocols:** When your group or company uses GMRS radios, make sure that everyone knows how to talk to each other clearly and concisely. Set normal rules for how to start and end conversations, such as signal codes, channel assignments, and emergency processes. Using clear communication rules cuts down on uncertainty and boosts productivity in tough scenarios.

- **Routine Equipment Testing**: Test and maintain your GMRS radio equipment regularly to make sure it works properly. Check the stability of important parts like batteries, radios, and mics to find problems quickly. It is important to fix any problems right away so that contact stays effective.

- **Effective Emergency Preparedness:** Get ready for accidents by practicing emergencies and doing drills daily. Your team should practice using crisis signs, planning how to respond, and following emergency procedures. Evaluate success and find ways to make things better so that you are better prepared for and able to handle real situations.

- **Bringing Essential Supplies:** If you're going to be outside or in a remote area with a GMRS radio, make sure you bring the supplies you need to stay safe and healthy. Bring things like water, food, first aid tools, and a place to stay in case of an accident or a delay. Being well-equipped makes you more resilient and ready for tough scenarios.

- **Professional Training**: Look into professional training options in radio contact and emergency planning to improve your skills and knowledge. There are a lot of groups that give classes and certificates in radio handling, emergency response, and survival in the wild. Getting professional training gives you the skills and knowledge you need to handle situations well.

Chapter 8

GMRS Radio in Outdoor Activities

GMRS Radios for Hiking, Camping, and Backpacking

Hiking and camping are popular social activities, so bringing phones and other electronics may not be necessary to avoid becoming sidetracked. On the other hand, some places—like the woods, where camping and hiking are popular—make it impossible to have any type of connection, much alone the internet. Therefore, if you choose to bring your phones and devices, it could be challenging to communicate with them. However, emergencies might happen or communication with others is necessary, therefore it's important to know how to operate the GMRS radio even while trekking. Here are some pointers and what to keep in mind on how to use the GMRS radio and why it's so important while camping and hiking:

Improved Security and communication

In isolated outdoor locations with spotty or nonexistent mobile phone service, GMRS radios are dependable means of communication. The American Hiking Society states that staying in contact with your group or emergency services is essential to guaranteeing your safety while going on outdoor adventures. Hiking, camping, and backpacking are made safer by the use of GMRS radios, which provide a way to keep in touch and call for assistance in an emergency.

Furthermore, the National Park Service acknowledges the significance of GMRS radios as necessary safety equipment for exploring the wilderness. When camping in remote locations or trekking across difficult terrain, outdoor enthusiasts may stay in touch with other hikers or request help by carrying a GMRS radio.

Extended-Distance Communication

The capacity of GMRS radios to communicate over larger distances than FRS (Family Radio Service) radios is one of its main advantages. This feature is highlighted by OutdoorGearLab, which emphasizes how important it is for group members who are dispersed across huge regions to stay in touch with one another. Whether trekking on designated paths, camping in isolated areas or going off-trail, GMRS radios allow outdoor enthusiasts to maintain communication regardless of their distance.

The significance of GMRS radios' long-range communication capabilities is emphasized by the Wilderness Medical Society, especially in situations when hikers or backpackers run into unforeseen dangers or need rescue help. GMRS radios improve outdoor activity safety and coordination in a variety of situations by increasing communication range.

Environmental and Terrain Consideration

Although GMRS radios are capable of long-distance communication, climatic conditions, and topography may affect how successful they are. When using GMRS radios outdoors, outdoor enthusiasts need to consider these factors; mountainous terrain, dense foliage, and climatic conditions may all have an impact on the transmission range and power of a signal.

Hikers should be aware of their surroundings and modify their communication tactics appropriately, according to OutdoorGearLab. Finding wide spaces or high spots along the path may help with radio transmission and reception. Similarly, to maximize communication efforts and prepare for any signal interruptions, the Appalachian Trail Conservancy advises becoming acquainted with the hiking route's terrain.

Power management and battery life

It's important to take power management and battery life into account while utilizing GMRS radios for outdoor activities. Backpacker.com suggests using GMRS radios with lengthy battery lives or the ability to use rechargeable batteries to reduce the possibility of running out of power on longer trips. Keeping extra batteries on hand or investing in a portable solar charger may also assist reduce battery-related problems.

The Outdoor Life magazine highlights the need to preserve battery life by reducing pointless transmissions and modifying transmission power levels, in line with communication requirements and ambient factors. Outdoor enthusiasts may guarantee that their GMRS radios stay functional throughout their trips by using effective power management procedures.

Emergency Response and Preparation

During outdoor expeditions, GMRS radios are essential for emergency planning and response. Along with other necessities like first aid supplies, an emergency shelter, and signaling devices, the American Red Cross urges hikers and campers to include GMRS radios in their emergency preparation packs. GMRS radios provide a dependable means of communication in an emergency, allowing users to coordinate with rescue services or ask other outdoor enthusiasts for aid.

Before setting out on an outdoor excursion, Wilderness Medical Associates International emphasizes how important it is to create emergency communication procedures and practice using them. Hikers and backpackers may become more prepared for unanticipated circumstances by practicing distress signals, emergency frequencies, and response protocols via the use of fake scenarios.

Logistics and Group Coordination

During outdoor events, GMRS radios help with efficient group coordination and logistics. GMRS radios provide instantaneous communication among team members, optimizing safety procedures, streamlining decision-making procedures, and guaranteeing that all members remain informed and linked. Backpacker magazine suggests setting up specific frequencies or channels for group chat in order to reduce noise and maximize effectiveness.

Moreover, rendezvous locations, navigation updates, and plan or route modifications may all be sent using GMRS radios. This degree of communication fosters camaraderie, collaboration, and mutual support among participants, which improves the outdoor adventure experience as a whole.

Boating and Maritime Applications

The GMRS radios are essential for boating and marine applications. When navigating waterways, these radios provide a dependable communication option that is critical for safety, coordination, and emergency response. The following are tips you need to keep in mind;

Security and Emergency Communication

When it comes to guaranteeing safety and enabling emergency communication on the water, GMRS radios are essential. The United States Coast Guard (USCG) asserts that keeping lines of communication open and functional is critical to averting mishaps, handling crises, and organizing rescue efforts. With GMRS radios, boaters may communicate directly with other boats, marinas, and emergency services, allowing them to report emergencies or seek help promptly.

Every vessel should have a communication device, such as a GMRS radio, on board, according to the National Safe Boating Council. When an emergency arises, such as a medical emergency, accident, or navigational danger, boaters may efficiently organize rescue operations, send out distress signals, and convey vital information by using GMRS radios. GMRS radios improve boaters' and their passengers' safety and security while navigating waterways by offering a dependable communication channel.

Extended-Distance Communication Abilities

When compared to other maritime communication equipment like mobile phones or VHF radios, GMRS radios have a longer communication range. Boating Magazine notes that GMRS radios have greater power levels and longer transmission ranges, which make them appropriate for boaters traveling across vast bodies of water or visiting isolated locations with spotty cell phone service.

For boaters that operate in locations with limited VHF coverage or wander beyond the range of VHF radios, the BoatUS Foundation recommends GMRS radios. While out on the water, GMRS radios provide boaters with a dependable way to communicate over long distances, enabling them to keep in contact with marinas, harbormasters, and other boats. This increased range provides connection even in isolated or offshore places and improves situational awareness.

Weather Surveillance and Warnings

Boaters and their boats are in danger from abrupt changes in the weather, which has a big impact on boating safety. Boaters may safeguard their safety by making educated judgments and taking appropriate action based on timely weather updates and alerts provided by GMRS radios equipped with weather alert functions.

The National Weather Service (NWS) advises boaters to use the weather alert systems on GMRS radios or tune in to NOAA Weather Radio broadcasts to be updated about the weather. Boaters may reduce risks by planning their journeys in accordance with the latest meteorological information, which helps them avoid possible dangers including thunderstorms, strong winds, and choppy seas. Boaters can keep ahead of shifting weather patterns and take proactive measures to address weather-related concerns while they're out on the water thanks to weather notifications sent by GMRS radios.

Protocols for Communication and Channel Selection

Maintaining effective and transparent communication when out on the water requires careful channel selection and adherence to established norms. To reduce interference and guarantee efficient coordination, the United States Power Squadrons (USPS) advise using approved channels for certain activities, including distress calls, regular communications, or vessel-to-vessel contact.

The USPS Boating Course places a strong emphasis on being acquainted with the communication protocols and channel assignments provided by regional maritime authorities. Boaters may improve safety and operational efficiency on the water by adhering to established norms and utilizing the proper channels to maintain clear contact with other boats, marinas, and emergency services.

Help with Navigation and Coordination

GMRS radios let boats coordinate and receive navigational aid, especially in crowded ports or active waterways. To lower the chance of collisions or accidents, the USCG Navigation Center emphasizes the need for good communication when communicating navigational objectives, asking for passage, or issuing warnings to other boats.

Boating World magazine suggests coordinating operations in confined locations or small waterways utilizing GMRS radios for bridge-to-bridge communication. Boaters may navigate securely and effectively, reducing disturbances and guaranteeing smooth passage across crowded waters, by keeping lines of communication open. GMRS radios are vital instruments for keeping sailors aware of their surroundings and encouraging safe navigation.

Off-Roading and Outdoor Adventures with GMRS

As you know, dependable communication is a must while off-roading. Even in places where there is cell coverage, mobile phones are often not a viable solution for constant communication between cars while 'wheeling. The off-road community has been using GMRS radios for decades, this is partially because there are a ton of GMRS radio options available at a variety of budgets. Additionally, GMRS may access repeaters to significantly extend communication range and perhaps enable you to call for assistance in an emergency if mobile phone coverage is not available.

Choosing a GMRS radio is comparable to choosing your 4x4's locking differential. Hence, similar to the abundance of lockers available on the market, GMRS radios are also widely available, with varying features and prices. You must decide how you want to use the radio and how much money you are willing to invest.

"Handy-talkies' ' or "HTs" as they are often called in the radio industry make up the great bulk of GMRS radios available on the market. These most likely differ from the walkie-talkies you used to play with as a child. These are substantially more feature-rich and have transmit powers of between two and five watts. GMRS HTs vary in price from being low-cost and simple to being what's often called "prosumer," meaning they have all the bells and whistles but at a greater cost. With the detachable antenna feature of some GMRS HTs, you may enhance the broadcast and receive range by upgrading the antenna or adding a stubby one for usage in confined spaces. To extend range, connect the majority of radios with detachable antenna to an external antenna (such as a magnet-mount antenna on your 4x4). While some HTs may be charged without a dock, some include a charge connector that makes charging while on the move simpler. Some may greatly extend the transmission range by acting as repeaters. Certain HTs include front panel and/or software customization options. In order to guarantee that they will function in unclean and/or damp environments, as those encountered while off-roading, certain radios are also IP-rated.

Additionally, there is a range of "mobile" 12-volt GMRS radios that may be used as base stations or in cars. Generally speaking, mobile radios provide much greater ERP than HTs (up to the GMRS 50-watt max limit), this may result in a wider spectrum of communication. Similar to HTs, there are many different types of mobile radios available today, ranging from prosumer to basic. A key point to remember is that a 50-watt GMRS radio will often have a longer range than a radio with a lower power output, but because of its high amp draw, it must be connected directly to your

4x4's battery. However, because of their lower amp demand, some of the lower-power GMRS mobile radios may be powered by the 12-volt power outlet in your car, and the majority of them have a power plug placed on the wire.

Antenna Significance

Selecting a GMRS radio is not the only step toward successful off-road communication. To optimize radio performance, the second half consists of selecting a high-quality antenna and installing it appropriately. An example of this would be putting a powerful big-block engine inside your 4x4 and then connecting it to an exhaust system that is too small and not properly routed, or a high-output GMRS radio coupled to a low-quality or incorrectly positioned antenna. If you do not do this, your radio would not be performing at its best, just as the engine performance of your 4x4 would suffer.

Numerous GMRS-tuned antennas with high dB gain and premium coaxial wire are available. Certain ones (like the metal roof on your 4x4) need a ground plane, while others don't. There are also several ways to attach an antenna; the one you choose will depend on the kind of 4x4 you have and the surface (fake, metal, or aluminum) you want to put the antenna on. It's crucial to mount your radio's antenna as high on your car as you can if you want to increase its range. You should always have in mind that, in the world of antennas, height equals might. Also, the location and method of 'wheeling' will determine if a high-mount antenna is feasible.

Repeaters and GMRS

Several GMRS radios have the amazing ability to use repeaters to significantly extend their transmission range. To put it simply, radio transmissions on one frequency are normally received by most GMRS repeater systems, amplified, and then sent on a different frequency. In order to maximize receive and broadcast range, repeater antennas are often positioned on buildings, towers, hills, or mountaintops (height does matter when it comes to antennas). Since GMRS is a line-of-sight communication technology, impediments often restrict its range.

To know how important a repeater is during off-roading, consider the following scenario: assume that you are off-roading and unable to obtain cell service and there is a need for you to chat with a fellow four-wheeler who is five miles away, but there is a mountain in between you. There will be no communication since the mountain blocks your GMRS signal. This is an example of where the importance of a repeater during off roading, comes to play. On the other hand, your range may be greatly expanded if there is a repeater on that mountain. It can receive your radio signal, amplify it, and retransmit it. Also note that the distance you can communicate with a repeater depends on several variables, such as your height, obstacles in your path, the antenna's altitude, your radio's output power, the repeater's output power, and meteorological conditions. Best example: A repeater may enable you to communicate with another GMRS radio that is located 30 miles north of it if its range is 30 miles in a circular radius and your radio can reach it at its southernmost point. Undoubtedly, the total range of 60 miles is noteworthy.

While many GMRS radios can be used with repeaters, not all of them can, so be sure the GMRS radio you're buying can use repeaters if that's your preference. Repeater-capable GMRS radios often feature channel options that allow them to broadcast on the repeater's input frequency and receive on its output frequency. They will also typically be identified as such by the manufacturer. GMRS radios with repeater functionality will now have the option to choose and broadcast the repeater's "PL tone," which grants access to the repeater. The subaudible PL tone allows your radio signal to be received by the repeater's input side. Do not forget, the repeater will not enable your radio transmission to be accepted if this PL tone is not heard.

Chapter 9

GMRS Radio for Family and Group Communication

Family Communication Strategies with GMRS

In order to ensure everyone's safety, happiness, and cooperation throughout different group activities and events, family communication is important. Effective communication techniques are essential whether you're arranging an outdoor excursion, a family get-together, or just a day trip. To optimize efficiency and effectiveness, there are some important tactics and best practices you may use while utilizing GMRS (General Mobile Radio Service) radios for family communication. They have been provided below:

Selection of Frequencies

When using GMRS radios, choosing the right frequency is essential for clear communication. It's crucial to look up the channels that are accessible in your area before you go and choose one that has the least amount of interference. Reliability of communication may be improved by organizing with family members to decide on a certain channel or channels. Avoiding crowded frequencies can help you reduce interference and guarantee that your communications are received clearly.

Channel Monitoring

It is imperative that you encourage family members to continuously watch the chosen GMRS channel(s) throughout your activity or event. Frequent monitoring makes sure that everyone stays in contact and is aware of any developments, plans, or potential emergencies. A feeling of togetherness and safety is fostered among the group when members periodically check in with each other, especially if they are exploring various regions or participating in distinct activities.

Unambiguous Communication Protocol

Developing a clear communication protocol is essential to facilitating productive communication via GMRS radios. Creating standard words, codes, or signals for often occurring communications, such as "Check-in time," "Need assistance," or "Emergency," streamlines communication and reduces confusion, particularly in emergencies when prompt and accurate replies are critical.

Designated Leaders

Identifying leaders or points of contact within your family group facilitates decision-making and communication. Assign one or more people to the role of leader, who will be in charge of organizing communication and directing the group during any outside activities or events. A feeling of direction and security inside the group is fostered by clearly defined leadership responsibilities, which guarantee that everyone knows whom to turn to for orders, support, or updates.

Procedures for Check-In

Establishing consistent check-in protocols fosters responsibility and improves the security of every member of the family. Set up designated check-in times or intervals during which each participant updates the group on their whereabouts and current state. This procedure makes it easier to recognize any problems or crises quickly, allowing for fast support or action when needed.

Being Ready for Emergencies

It's important to acquaint family members with emergency protocols and procedures before starting any activity. Make sure that everyone knows how to use any emergency features on GMRS radios, how to signal for aid, and what to do in the event of an accident or separation. Family members may be better prepared for unforeseen circumstances and reinforced in acceptable reaction procedures by participating in emergency exercises or simulations.

Practice Session

To make sure that everyone is comfortable using GMRS radios and adhering to communication regulations, regular practice sessions are essential. Introduce family members to the capabilities and operations of the radios, such as station switching, setting up notifications for the weather, and using privacy codes. Practice sessions may be used to simulate different circumstances, which facilitates the rehearsing of emergency replies and the assessment of the efficacy of communication tactics.

Management of Battery

GMRS radios need proper battery management in order to function continuously. Make sure all radios are fully charged and have extra batteries or power sources before starting any activity. Check battery levels often throughout the day to avoid unplanned power outages and to ensure constant communication, particularly on long excursions or in emergencies.

Weather Monitoring

It is essential to stay up to date on weather conditions and modify communication arrangements as necessary. GMRS radios may provide family members with weather warnings and updates, increasing their safety while engaging in outdoor activities. Keeping an eye on shifting weather patterns enables prompt plan revisions or the application of necessary safety measures.

Privacy Codes

If your GMRS radios support them, using privacy codes **(CTCSS/DCS)** reduces interference from other users on the same channel. By sifting out undesirable transmissions, privacy codes improve the secrecy of family conversations and guarantee that messages stay private and safe. Setting up privacy codes on each radio in your group ensures uninterrupted communication at all times.

Role Assignment

Giving each family member distinct duties and obligations encourages a feeling of responsibility and ownership. Assign work appropriately to those who excel in first aid, communication, navigation, or other pertinent abilities. Having clearly defined duties helps everyone contribute to the success of the group and distributes the job fairly, which lowers stress and promotes better coordination.

Listening Techniques

Instruct family members on the value of active listening techniques. To make sure that everyone hears and comprehends information correctly, encourage careful listening. Try summarizing or paraphrasing communications to make sure you understand them and to quickly clear up any confusion. In a family group, listening well fosters understanding between members and improves communication efficacy in general.

Flexibility and Adaptability

Keep your communication style fluid and adaptive, particularly in circumstances that are unforeseen or dynamic. As situations change, be ready to modify your communication strategy, tactics, or responsibilities. Family members should be encouraged to have an open mind and to be flexible, seeing obstacles or changes as chances for personal development. Being adaptable builds resilience and makes it easier for the family unit to deal with unforeseen challenges or changes.

Feedback and Reflection

To continually enhance communication methods and procedures, family members should be encouraged to reflect and provide feedback. Spend some time discussing what went well, what may be better, and any lessons that were learned after each activity or event. Get feedback from all parties involved in order to get a variety of viewpoints and pinpoint areas that want improvement. Thinking back on previous experiences helps the family group communicate more effectively and promotes ongoing progress.

Applying Communication Tools

Use various technologies and communication tools in addition to GMRS radios to improve coordination and connection. Particularly in places with spotty radio coverage, think about augmenting radio communication with mobile applications, GPS units, or messaging services. The possibility of effective communication is increased and redundancy is ensured when numerous communication channels are integrated, especially in difficult or distant situations.

Group Activities and Events Coordination

Using GMRS radios to coordinate group activities and events may significantly improve communication effectiveness and overall organization. GMRS radios provide a dependable way to keep everyone in the loop, whether you're organizing a neighborhood event, organizing a family reunion, or organizing a camping trip. Here's how to coordinate events and group activities using GMRS radios:

Getting Ready and Making Plans

For group activities and events to be effective, there has to be enough planning and preparation. Start by describing the goals, parameters, and schedule of the event. Decide which important people will take on the role of designated leaders or coordinators in charge of overseeing communication initiatives. Choose the right GMRS channels and frequencies based on the number of people in the group, possible interference, and local laws.

Channel Designation

For various uses, such as subgroup coordination, emergency communication, and public notifications, designate distinct GMRS channels or frequencies. Make sure that everyone is aware of the channel assignments and knows which channels are appropriate for different kinds of communication. To reduce interference and improve the secrecy of group conversations, think about using privacy codes (CTCSS/DCS).

Group Instruction

Before the event, provide a thorough group briefing to go over emergency protocols, channel allocations, and communication protocols. Give participants a rundown of how GMRS radios work, including how to choose a channel, how to utilize extra features like privacy codes and weather warnings, and basic functioning. Make sure that everyone knows how to use GMRS radios correctly and is aware of their function in promoting communication during the event.

Specific Leaders

Assign team members or leaders to oversee communication within certain regions or groups. These people need to have GMRS radios and be well-versed in information relaying, activity coordination, and emergency response protocols. As focal points for dialogue and decision-making, designated leaders facilitate efficient collaboration and guarantee clear communication.

Procedures for Check-In

Establish consistent check-in protocols to uphold responsibility and guarantee every participant's safety throughout the event. Establish predefined check-in periods or intervals during which participants use the GMRS radios to communicate their position, status, and other pertinent information. Check-in protocols aid in tracking people's locations, identifying problems or concerns, and facilitating prompt assistance when required.

Distress Call

Establish a precise procedure for responding to and communicating in an emergency. Make sure everyone is aware of how to call for assistance, start an emergency broadcast, and provide emergency responders with pertinent information. Establish preset emergency codes or signals for prompt identification and response, and designate certain channels or frequencies for emergency communication. To guarantee preparedness and efficiency in an emergency, review and perform emergency protocols regularly.

Activity Coordination

Throughout the event, use GMRS radios to coordinate different duties and activities. Assign distinct channels or frequencies to various activity groups or teams, including personnel responsible for setup, transportation, and entertainment. Promote instantaneous communication across teams to guarantee seamless synchronization, prompt modifications, and efficient resolution of issues. Urge participants to behave sensibly while using GMRS radios by refraining from superfluous talk or interfering with important lines of communication.

Weather Surveillance

Use GMRS radios to inform participants of weather updates and advisories, particularly for outdoor activities. Assign individuals or groups the task of keeping an eye on the weather and informing the group on time. Keep an eye out for variations in the weather and be ready to modify plans or take the necessary safety steps when necessary. Disseminate weather-related information and plan reactions to unfavorable weather circumstances by using GMRS radios.

Constant Communication

Throughout the event, keep lines of communication open and constant to handle any concerns, offer updates, and encourage participant involvement. Urge participants to respect established communication procedures, refrain from needless chatter, and avoid interfering with vital communication channels while using GMRS radios. Encourage a proactive communication culture where people are encouraged to share knowledge and provide assistance to one another when required.

After-Event Analysis

Hold a comprehensive post-event debriefing session to assess the success of your communication plan and pinpoint areas that need improvement. Ask participants about their thoughts on GMRS radios, communication procedures, and general coordinating efforts. Utilize this input to improve participant experience overall and your communication plan for the next events.

Chapter 10

Advanced GMRS Radio Features and Technologies

GPS Integration and Location Tracking

GMRS radios with GPS and position tracking built-in may greatly improve group activities and event organization, safety, and communication effectiveness. Users of GPS technology may locate themselves precisely, communicate their position in real-time to others, and navigate successfully even in difficult-to-reach places.

GPS Integration Benefits

- **Increased Safety**: Participants may communicate their exact position with others, which speeds up replies in case of emergencies or other circumstances when help is needed.

- **Better Coordination:** Leaders can keep an eye on everyone's whereabouts and make well-informed judgments by using real-time monitoring to monitor participant positions.

- **Effective Navigation**: By using GPS capabilities, participants may travel to designated waypoints, landmarks, or meeting locations, which lowers the possibility of getting lost and guarantees that everyone remains on track.

GPS- Enabled GMRS Radios

- It should be noted that not all GMRS radios have this function. GMRS radios with GPS, on the other hand, include integrated receivers that use signals from GPS satellites to identify the device's geographic coordinates.

- These radios often show location data on the screen, enabling users to monitor progress, check their current position, and navigate to pre-established waypoints or destinations.

Location Tracking Features

- **Real-Time Position Reporting:** GMRS radios with GPS capabilities may provide other group members with real-time position updates. This feature makes it possible to follow people's whereabouts continuously, improving safety and situational awareness.

- **Waypoint Navigation**: Using GPS guidance, users may use their GMRS radios to specify waypoints or locations and then travel to them. During group events, this capability is especially helpful for directing participants to designated sites or meeting spots.

- **Geo-Fencing**: This feature lets users designate virtual borders or safe zones and is supported by some GMRS radios with GPS capability. The radio may automatically notify the user or other group members when a participant enters or leaves a preset region, adding an extra layer of security and monitoring capabilities.

Combining Map-Related Software

- Users of GPS-enabled GMRS radios may obtain comprehensive maps, satellite imaging, and topographical data via seamless integration with mapping software or mobile apps.

- By giving users visual representations of the surrounding region, important sites of interest, and possible dangers, these mapping applications improve situational awareness and navigation.

Group Communication and Position Sharing

- GMRS radios facilitate seamless communication and coordination by allowing participants to request the positions of other group members, ensuring continuous connectivity and situational awareness.

- Participants can share their current position with other group members, allowing leaders to track everyone's positions in real time and make informed decisions accordingly.

- Rescue teams can quickly locate and assist people, even in remote or inaccessible areas, by using the GPS coordinates provided by the radios to expedite response efforts and ensure timely assistance. GPS-enabled GMRS radios are invaluable tools for transmitting distress signals along with precise location information in an emergency.

Weather Alerts and NOAA Channels

Do you know that with the GMRS radio, you can see incoming weather status? Also, for the purpose of better understanding, The **Retevis RA86 GMRS Tractor Radio has been used to give a step-by-step analysis, although the steps are relatively the same for other radios. Follow through below;**

You can get fast NOAA weather information with the weather alert and NOAA weather prediction on the Retevis RA86 GMRS Tractor Radio, which is more dependable than a cell phone. This is because, with about 10 NOAA weather channels, the Retevis RA86 GMRS Tractor Radio ensures you never miss any weather updates.

Weather forecast channel frequency table

Channel	RX	Channel	RX
1	162.5500	6	162.5000
2	162.4000	7	162.5250
3	162.4750	8	161.6500
4	162.4250	9	161.7750
5	162.4500	10	163.2750

Your Retevis RA86 GMRS Tractor Radio also has a NOAA Weather Alert feature that you can enable to get timely weather notifications. This feature helps you plan for agricultural tasks like planting, irrigation, harvesting, and so on, as well as to minimize losses.

Set NOAA for Retevis RA86 GMRS Tractor Radio

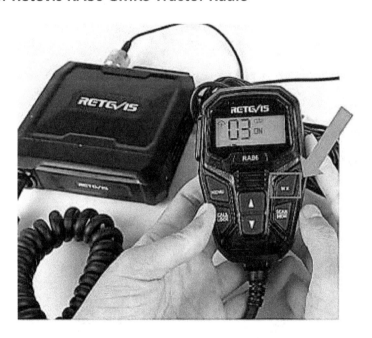

By using the **WX key**, you may enable the Retevis RA86 GMRS Tractor Radio to immediately access the NOAA weather scan from the GMRS channel.

In order to notify you of updates about severe weather, NOAA Weather search will automatically search the ten available **Weather (WX)** band channels and lock onto the strongest weather channel.

When the device is in scanning mode for weather forecasts, pause at the weather channel where the signal is received.

Additionally, you may change the weather station by quickly pressing the microphone's plus and minus channel buttons. To leave the weather mode, press and hold the **PTT button** or briefly press the **WX** button once again.

Configure the NOAA Weather Alert for Retevis RA86 GMRS Tractor Radio

When the Retevis RA86 GMRS Tractor Radio is in the weather forecast scanning mode, it is possible to change the weather channel using the channel key and simultaneously switch off the weather forecast scanning function and turn on the squelch by briefly pressing the **Scan/Mon button.**

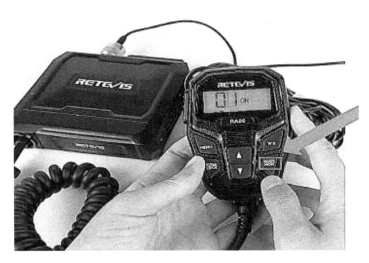

To access the weather forecast alarm switch setting, briefly press the **MENU button** after selecting the desired alarm channel. If there is a possibility of severe weather in your location, a NOAA Weather Alert will sound.

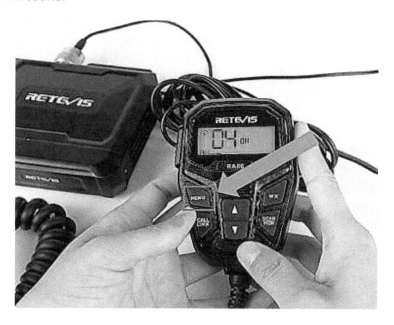

To finish configuring and go back to the weather channel, choose **ON/OFF** using the volume keys, then press and hold the **MENU button** once again.

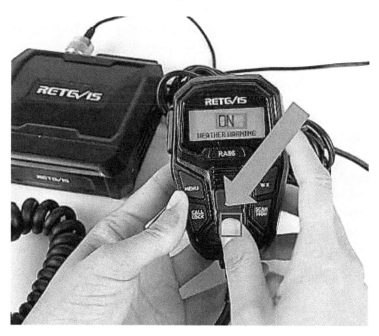

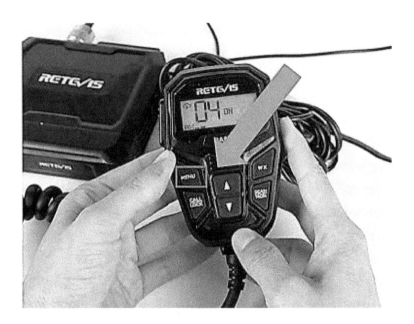

When the alarm feature is turned on:

- Any channel that receives 1050 HZ alarm modulation will cause the weather forecast alarm to sound while Retevis RA86 is in weather channel mode.

- The weather channel that Retevis RA86 will monitor is the one before the user exits the weather forecast. Note, this happens while it is on the GMR channel.

Encryption and Privacy Features

The method of encrypting information (in this example, audio signals) so that authorized parties may access it but eavesdroppers or hackers cannot decipher it is known as encryption. Using a coding mechanism, encryption in GMRS radios changes a speech transmission; an encryption key controls this algorithm. In order to receive broadcasts, all radios that are communicating need to have matching encryption keys.

There are several techniques for encrypting voice communications, and they have been explained below;

Basic Inversion Encryption

Note; that the speech signal's frequencies and loudness are reversed during inversion scrambling.

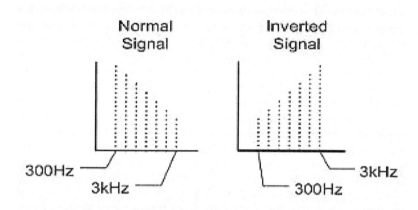

All of the 300 Hz voice signal frequencies and the loudness level are inverted to 3 kHz in the illustration above. The majority of GMRS radios with basic voice inversion provide 32 distinct encryption keys for selection. Also, using software for radio programming, the radio's keys are programmed. Your communications will only be received by radios that are within signal range, are operating on the same frequency, and have the same encryption key, privacy code, and privacy code. Most users of GMRS radios are sufficiently protected by this form of encryption, and this kind of built-in encryption is included in a lot of entry-level and mid-tier radios.

Encryption using Hopping Inversion

Compared to basic inversion, frequency hopping encryption offers a higher level of security. The picture below illustrates how the frequencies and frequency rates fluctuate while using this strategy.

In consequence, the speech signal begins to "hop" among various frequencies and frequency rates. While most commercial radios do not employ this technology, some have in the 900MHz band.

Encryption using Rolling Code Inversion

The speech signal is inverted using a technique called rolling code inversion, which varies the rate of inversion continuously. The signal ascends to the top limit after beginning at an upward inversion frequency direction, as shown in the image below.

Once it hits the lower limit, it then changes course and inverts at lower frequencies. Unlike basic voice inversion, it is a more secure kind of encryption. With rolling code encryption, the majority of radios provide 1020 encryption keys for selection, and software is used to program the radio's keys. However, similar to basic inversion, your broadcasts can only be heard by radios that are within signal range, are operating on the same frequency, and have the same privacy code and encryption key. The number of codes (1020 for rolling) and the signal's "rolling" inversion, which makes it harder to break, are the two differences between rolling code and simple inversion. Note; for more delicate applications, the rolling code is used.

Note: The rolling code encryption function is an optional feature found on most sophisticated radios and certain mid-tier radios.

DES and AES Encryption

Most sensitive applications employ either AES (Advanced Encryption Standard) or its cousin DES (Data Encryption Standard). Examples of these applications include the FBI, the military, and some banking applications. DES was created in the 1970s, but in many applications, its more recent relative AES has taken its place. These encryption algorithms are quite sophisticated, and their whole explanation requires some knowledge of mathematics and encryption techniques.

How AES and DES Encryption Keys Are Set

Setting the encryption keys for AES and DES is very delicate as they are used in highly sensitive applications. A unique tool called a "**Keyloader,**" often referred to as a KVL (Key Variable Loader), is needed to set the codes. The operator may input the keys into the encryption boards inside each radio by using this gadget, which resembles a radio. Through the use of a unique cable, the KVL is connected to the radio by connecting to the interface port. Depending on the protocol, the operator inputs individual digits and letters into the KVL to generate a special code for your radio communication. Your code, which consists of around 20 characters, is transcribed by the KVL into the final key that is inserted into each radio. These devices are kept under strict security at radio shops or government organizations, where they are kept, since access to the KVL grants access to the whole system.

Handling Encryption Keys in a Complicated Environment

So, when you have a massive operation, how do you manage to alter the encryption keys? The solution is called **OTAR (Over-The-Air-Rekeying).** The encryption keys in OTAR are centrally managed by a specialized computer known as a Key Management Controller (KMC). As the name implies, OTAR enables fresh encryption keys to be loaded into radios over the air. Moreover, encryption keys may be removed remotely. All of the system's radios, excluding the lost one, may be rekeyed over the air in the event of a radio theft or loss. Furthermore, in the event that you unintentionally remove your radio's battery, wiping out the encryption key, the KMC can remotely download the key back into your device. To facilitate the transportation of encryption keys, the KMC can download the keys into KVLs. In the event that the radios are outside the KMC's coverage area, the KVL gadget might serve as a substitute.

Although, one encryption key at a time can be stored on most radios. However, certain radios may also store more than one encryption key (multi-key). Multi-key enables selected users to have both encryption keys in their radios to communicate with both groups while they are using distinct encryption keys, keeping the other members of the group from listening in on their talks. Also, up to 16 distinct encryption keys may be stored in some GMRS radios.

Note: Generally speaking, multi-key and OTAR are limited to more sophisticated radio models.

Encryption Compatibility Across Different Brands

Sometimes people often ask, what radio brands are compatible with each other's encryption. The short answer is that the only standardized encryption techniques are **DES and AES**. This indicates that various two-way radio brands are compatible with AES and DES. On the other hand, no established guidelines exist for rolling code inversion or basic inversion encryption. For both rolling and basic code inversion, each manufacturer is free to use their codes and scrambling strategies. Therefore, rolling code inversion encryption and basic inversion encryption are often incompatible between brands.

Chapter 11

Troubleshooting and Maintenance

Common Issues and Solutions

Issues with charging

Many people see a steady yellow or orange light when they put their batteries in the charger for the first time to charge them. This is an automatic cleaning that is meant to extend the life of your battery by draining it completely and then charging it again. It takes 12 hours to do this.

A lot of people make the mistake of using the radio at this time, but it will drain your battery. The radio needs to go through this cycle all the way through until you see a consistent green light. This means the radio is fully charged.

You can stop this automatic cleaning process by setting your charge to "**rapid charge**"; put the radio in the charger once, take it out quickly, and then put it back in the charger again.

The radio's light will then change from a steady orange light to a steady red light. This means it's starting to charge quickly.

This is what the Radio's charging lights mean:

Charge Indicator	Description
SINGLE GREEN FLASH	Charger has 100% power
FLASHING RED	Battery is not making proper contact with the charger
FLASHING ORANGE	Battery is recognized by charger but is waiting to charge. (Either the battery voltage is too low or the battery temperature is too low or too high to allow charging. When this condition is corrected, the battery will automatically begin charging)
STEADY RED	Battery is in rapid charge mode
FLASHING GREEN	Battery has completed rapid charge to 90% capacity. Leave in charger to complete the charge.

STEADY GREEN	Battery has completed charging and is 100% charged.
FLASHING RED/GREEN	Battery has completed charging and is fully charged. Battery continues to be useable, but may be nearing the end of its rated service life.
STEADY ORANGE	Battery is in recondition or initialization mode. The length of time the charger remains in this mode depends upon the state of charge remaining in the battery when inserted. (Fully charged batteries require more time to recondition, 8 to 12 hours or more, than fully discharged batteries)

What to do when you are experiencing delay or lag?

When there is a delay or lag, usually, it is often a **user error**; you probably aren't holding down the **push-to-talk (PTT) button** long enough. Remember that you have to hold it down the whole time you talk.

Also, some people forget to let go of it when they're done, which can also mess up communication.

Other Users aren't able to hear your transmission because you're cutting out

Can't the people on the other end of the radio hear you? Are the sounds losing their place?

People often start talking as soon as they press the PTT button, but you should wait a second to make sure you don't lose the first few words.

Also, most of the time, people are either too close or too far away from the mic, or they talk too loudly or too low. You should be about 3 inches away from the microphone and speak normally; also, don't talk too fast.

In some cases, you may have broken the antenna, so look to see if there are any dents or bends, because this can also make transmissions go wrong.

Your Radio Cuts Out too often or you are having trouble with coverage (dead spots)

- **Are you trying to communicate through concrete?**

In general, coverage can be affected by the number of floors and stairways, as well as the length of the stairs. To put it another way, you won't be able to communicate with another user from a concrete parking lot. So, before you do anything else, look at the areas where you're having trouble with service.

- **Do You Use a Concrete Analog**

An analog radio doesn't have nearly as much range or sound quality as a digital GMRS radio. For the most part, digital radios cover 40% more ground than old stations.

Your earplugs are coming off

You can change to a different kind of earpiece or spying kit if this is happening to you. You should keep in mind that there are more than one kind of earphones, some just fit inside the ear, others have plastic parts that go around the ear, and still others have jelly parts that form to the inside of the ear.

Bad sound quality

The sound coming out is warped, weak, or cracking.

What to do:

- Make sure the noise settings are set correctly by checking them.
- Check the connections on the speaker or headset for any damage or broken connections.
- Clean the headset jack or speaker grille to get rid of any dirt or other things that are in the way.
- If you're using an external speaker or headset, try a different one to see if the problem is with that one.

Interference or Static Noise

During broadcasts, the radio picks up annoying disturbances or static noise.

Quick fix:

- Change the channel or frequency so that other users or sources don't mess with you.
- Change the silence settings to get rid of weak signals and lower the noise in the background.
- Move to a new spot or change where the antenna is placed to get a better signal.
- Look around for electrical gadgets or sources of interference, and if you can, move.

Coverage or Range is Limited

The radio doesn't cover as much area as I thought it would.

What you should do:

- Make sure the antenna on the radio is fully stretched and facing straight.
- Stay away from things that could block the radio signal, like houses, hills, or lots of trees.
- If the radio's output power can be changed, turn it up, but keep local laws and battery life in mind.
- If you want to communicate better in places with poor service, you might want to use a booster station.

Quick Battery Drain

The radio's batteries die quickly and need to be replaced often.

Solution:

- Use the high-quality replaceable batteries that the maker suggests.
- To save battery life, turn off features that aren't needed, like lights or scans.
- Keep the radio somewhere cool and dry when not in use to keep it from discharging too much.
- To get the most out of your batteries, replace old or worn-out ones with new ones.

Programming Errors

The radio's broadcast options are wrong or not working right.

Do the following:

- To learn how to return the radio to its original settings, look at the user manual or programming software.
- Check the programming settings again to make sure they are correct. This includes making sure the frequencies, channels, and secret codes are set properly.
- If you need to update the radio, use a suitable programming wire and software and carefully follow the manufacturer's directions.

Controls are Unresponsive

When you press the buttons or settings on the radio, nothing happens.

Quick Fix:

- Use a soft, dry cloth to clean the control panel and look around the buttons for dirt or moisture.
- To reset the radio, take out the batteries or unplug them for a few minutes and then put them back in.
- If the problem keeps happening, call the maker to get more help fixing it or finding a solution.

Inaccurate Display or screen problems

The radio's screen is fuzzy, flashing, or giving you the wrong information.

Follow these solutions:

- Change the settings for the screen, like the brightness or color, to make it easier to see.
- Check the screen for any scratches or other physical damage that might be making it hard to see.
- Reset the radio to its original settings to get rid of any software problems that might be causing the display to act strangely.

Antenna is Malfunctioning

The antenna on the radio is broken, missing, or not working properly.

What you should do:

- Look at the antenna for cracks or other obvious signs of wear and tear, and repair it if it needs to be.
- Make sure the antenna is properly adjusted and firmly connected to the radio's aerial port.
- If you want better signal receiving and broadcast range, you might want to consider getting a better antenna or one that is longer.

Frequency Drift or Problems with Drifting

The radio's frequency moves or changes without warning while it's being used.

Solution:

- Check the radio's frequency stability settings and make changes as needed to keep drift to a minimum.

- Don't put the radio in places with high temperatures or other factors that could change the frequency steadiness.
- If the problem keeps happening, get in touch with the maker or a trained expert to fix or calibrate it.

Routine Maintenance Practices

When GMRS radios break down, it's not always because of the radio itself, but because of how it's being used.

A lot of problems can be fixed by using radios the right way. Even though radios are supposed to be easy to use, you need some basic training and maintenance practices to use them.

Here are some common best practices tips and tricks to follow:

- While you are talking, hold the two-way radio two inches away from your mouth.
- Make sure people can hear you when you talk by speaking loudly.
- Hold down the PTT button until you're done talking to make sure that all of your texts get sent.

Make Maintenance a top priority

When you keep and take care of your GMRS radios the right way, they will last as long as possible. Taking care of your phone's battery and fixing it every day can also indirectly improve the sound quality.

As long as you follow these tips for maintaining your GMRS radios, you should be able to keep communicating without any problems for another five to seven years.

- If you want to charge your radio, remember to turn it off
- With a cotton cloth and a little water, clean the radio. It will remove dirt and smudges without damaging the unit because the cloth is soft. To get rid of tougher spots and marks, wipe the radios down with a damp cloth until they are clean.
- Radio antennas should not be held or grabbed. If you keep using the antenna as a handle, it will finally change how you send and receive signals.
- Only use chargers and batteries that work with the gadget. Once you've found extras that are made to work with your unit, keep them dry and only charge them when you need to. Batteries can lose power if they are overcharged.

The Best Way to Store/Keep Your Radio

- Before putting the radios away, turn them off and take the batteries out.

- Don't put batteries or radios away from active chargers.
- Keep in a dry, cool place that doesn't get too hot or cold or get too much sunlight or water.
- Keep radios and battery packs at 72° to avoid damage.

Chapter 12

Integrating GMRS Radios with Other Communication Systems

Compatibility with FRS (Family Radio Service) Radios

GMRS (General Mobile Radio Service) and FRS (Family Radio Service) are two popular radio contact services that are mostly used for communicating with family and friends. Knowing how GMRS and FRS radios work together can help people get the most out of their contact choices in these services. Here, we'll talk about the details of how GMRS and FRS radios can work together, including frequency range, power levels, channel assignment, legal requirements, compatibility, and interoperability.

How to Understand Frequency Range

Both GMRS and FRS radios work in the UHF (Ultra High Frequency) radio band, which in the US is usually between 462 MHz and 467 MHz. This frequency range is good for personal and family use because it allows for effective short-range contact.

Comparing Power Levels

When it comes to transmitting power, GMRS radios can use more than FRS radios. The most power that GMRS radios can use is 50 watts, while the most power that FRS radios can use is 2 watts. The difference in power flow has a big effect on the two services' ability to communicate and cover a large area.

Channel Allocation

In the UHF frequency band, both GMRS and FRS radios use the same channels. In the US, there are a total of 22 channels set aside for FRS/GMRS use. Each one has its frequency range and power limits. Channels 1 through 7 are only for FRS use, and the most power that can be sent is 0.5 watts. Channels 15–22 are only used for GMRS, which lets higher power levels happen. The FRS and GMRS services share channels 8–14, but FRS radios must use the lower power limit when they are on these channels.

Legal Requirements

The Federal Communications Commission (FCC) issues licenses for GMRS use, which covers the whole family. FRS, on the other hand, doesn't need a license and anyone can join. People with a

GMRS license can use both GMRS and FRS bands. People with an FRS license, on the other hand, can only use FRS channels and power levels.

Compatibility

When it comes to frequency range and available channels, GMRS radios and FRS radios usually work together. On the same FRS/GMRS bands, both types of radios can connect. However, differences in power generation may affect the quality and range of contact. For example, GMRS radios may be able to reach farther because they produce more power.

Making sure of Interoperability

The ability for GMRS and FRS radios to communicate with each other makes contact more flexible, especially in families or groups where people may have different types of radios. Users can converse well within the range limits of each radio type by using the channels that are shared by both GMRS and FRS services.

Interoperability with Amateur Radio (HAM) Systems

The ability of GMRS radios to work with Amateur Radio (HAM) radio systems is an interesting combination of different transmission methods. GMRS and HAM radio are both forms of radio transmission, but they have different rules for licenses, frequency bands, and how they should be used.

GMRS and HAM Radio Systems

Whereas, GMRS is an approved radio service that is mostly used for personal, short-distance calls. It works in the UHF frequency band and needs a license from the FCC to work.

On the other hand, HAM radio, or Amateur Radio, is a service for amateur radio operators that covers a wide range of frequencies, such as the HF, VHF, and UHF bands. To be a HAM, you need an amateur radio license from the FCC.

Frequency Bands and Licensing

GMRS works in the UHF range, usually between 462 and 467 MHz, and has special channel assignments and power limits. HAM radio, on the other hand, covers more frequency bands, such as HF, VHF, and UHF, giving approved users more ways to communicate.

Interoperability

Even though GMRS and HAM radio use different frequency bands and licensing systems, they can still work together and connect.

Also, cross-band repeaters and gateway systems can make it possible for GMRS and HAM radio systems to talk to each other, letting people join and work together across networks.

Cross-band Repeaters

GMRS and HAM radio users can communicate with each other through cross-band repeaters, which act as go-betweens for different radio systems. They take in signals on one frequency band, like GMRS, and send them again on a different band, like VHF or UHF HAM bands. Cross-band repeaters let GMRS and HAM radio users talk to each other, making the most of the best features of both systems.

Gateway Systems

Gateway devices work in a digital world but do the same thing that cross-band repeaters do. These systems connect the GMRS and HAM radio networks, making it easier for the two services to talk to each other and work together.

Also, Gateway managers set up their systems so that GMRS and HAM radio users can connect. This makes it easier for people to connect and work together.

Operational Considerations

Interoperability between GMRS and HAM radio systems is helpful, but users must follow the rules set by law and government. Also, GMRS users have to make sure they follow FCC rules about licenses, radio usage, and power limits.

HAM radio users must also stay within the frequency bands they are allowed to use and follow the rules set by the FCC for amateur radio.

Collaborative Projects and Events

GMRS and HAM radio users can work together on projects, events, and activities to get ready for emergencies, using both groups' tools and skills. For example, GMRS and HAM radio fans can work together at joint drills, field days, and community service events, which builds friendships and allows them to share their skills.

Integrating GMRS with Mobile Phones and Internet-Based Communication Platforms

It is becoming more common to connect GMRS to cell phones and internet-based systems. This combination not only makes standard radio contact more useful, but it also opens up new ways to meet, work together, and coordinate. Here are some examples of how you can connect your GMRS to other types of communication:

GMRS Radios and Bluetooth Connectivity

A lot of modern GMRS units have Bluetooth built-in, which lets them connect easily to cell phones and other Bluetooth-enabled devices. Users can get to a lot of different features by connecting the GMRS radio to a cell phone, such as:

- **Calls**: You can use your GMRS radio as a hands-free extension of your cell phone to make and receive calls. This makes it easy to stay in touch while you're busy.

- **Sending and getting text messages:** GMRS radios can add text messaging features by connecting a cell phone, which makes contact easier in places where voice communication might not be possible.

- **Using Internet-based communication apps**: When a person pairs their phone with a computer, the computer gives them access to the Internet. This means that they can use famous messaging apps like WhatsApp, Telegram, or Signal to make voice calls, send messages, and share media.

Voice Over Internet Protocol (VoIP) Integration

GMRS systems that can handle VoIP are another way to connect to networks that use the internet for communication. Users can connect their GMRS radios to systems like Zello, TeamSpeak, or Voxer by using VoIP technology, which will allow them to do the following:

- **Group communication**: On VoIP platforms, users can make virtual channels or chat rooms that let them talk to multiple people over the Internet without any problems.

- **Wider coverage:** Adding VoIP to GMRS contact makes it possible to talk over long distances via the internet, going beyond its normal coverage area.

- **Compatibility with a wide range of devices**: VoIP apps can be used on smartphones, tablets, and computers, giving users a choice of how to communicate.

Cross Band Repeaters

It is possible to communicate on different channels with cross-band repeaters, which act as links between GMRS radios and internet-based communication systems. These repeaters do the following:

- Get messages on one frequency band, like GMRS, and send them again on a different frequency band, like VHF/UHF or internet-based VoIP lines.

- Make GMRS communication more widespread by connecting radio signals to internet-based systems. This will allow people in different parts of the world to communicate with each other over long distances.

- Make it easier for GMRS radios and internet-based communication networks to work together, so people can talk to each other using a variety of technologies.

GMRS Radio Gateways for GMRS radios

GMRS Gateways connect GMRS radios to internet-based networks and allow connection between the two. Below are what the gateways do:

- Send voice calls, text messages, or other types of data between GMRS radios and platforms for online contact in real-time.
- Create a smooth link between old-fashioned radio communication and new internet-based technologies, making it easier for devices to talk to each other and connect.
- Increase the number of people who can use and reach GMRS communication by linking it to more communication platforms and networks.

Smartphone Apps that Support GMRS Integration

Smartphone apps that support GMRS integration make it easy for users to use GMRS contact features on their phones. Below are what these GMRS integrated Apps do:

- Make GMRS channels, bands, and transmission settings easy to get to through simple user interfaces.
- Allow users to interact easily with their smartphones by giving them features like channel scans, frequency selection, and text messaging.
- Make people more mobile and flexible by letting them use GMRS contact while they're on the go, without having to carry special radio gear.

Mobile Data Connection

GMRS radios can connect to cell phones or mobile hotspots to give users access to communication sites on the internet through a mobile data link:

- It lets GMRS radios connect to internet-based services like chat apps or VoIP apps over Wi-Fi or cellular data networks.
- Allows connection over long distances and in places where standard radio reception may be limited; gives you freedom of movement and flexibility.
- Allows for smooth communication between GMRS radio transmission and internet-based platforms, giving users a range of ways to communicate in different situations.

Integration with Dispatch Software

Syncing GMRS radios with dispatch software made for mobile devices and the internet makes it easier to handle and coordinate communications. What this does is:

- Creates a centralized method of communication for all communications that happen on different channels, like GMRS radios and networks that are based on the Internet.
- Make it easy to coordinate communication methods, such as voice calls, text messages, and info on where people are.
- Make better decisions and be more aware of what's going on by watching and analyzing conversation actions in real-time.